T0268859

THE
CRYSTAL
COMPANION

Quarto.com

© 2024 Quarto Publishing Group USA Inc.
Text © 2024 Rachel Hancock
Photography © 2022 Quarto Publishing Group USA Inc

First Published in 2024 by Fair Winds Press, an imprint of The Quarto Group,
100 Cummings Center, Suite 265-D, Beverly, MA 01915, USA.
T (978) 282-9590 F (978) 283-2742

Fair Winds Press titles are also available at discount for retail, wholesale, promotional, and bulk purchase. For details, contact the Special Sales Manager by email at specialsales@quarto.com or by mail at The Quarto Group, Attn: Special Sales Manager, 100 Cummings Center, Suite 265-D, Beverly, MA 01915, USA.

28 27 26 25 24   1 2 3 4 5

ISBN: 978-0-7603-9129-7

Digital edition published in 2024
eISBN: 978-0-7603-9130-3

This material was originally published under *The Ultimate Guide to Crystals: The Beginner's Guide to the Healing Energy of 100 Crystals and Stones* by Rachel Hancock (Fair Winds Press 2022).

Library of Congress Cataloging-in-Publication Data available under *The Ultimate Guide to Crystals: The Beginner's Guide to the Healing Energy of 100 Crystals and Stones* by Rachel Hancock.

Design: Amy Sly, The Sly Studio
Page Layout: Emily Austin, The Sly Studio
Photography: Rachel and Joel Hancock
Printed in China

The information in this book is for educational purposes only. It is not intended to replace the advice of a physician or medical practitioner. Please see your health-care provider before beginning any new health program.

THE
CRYSTAL
COMPANION

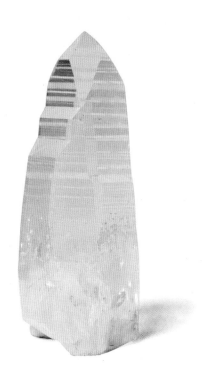

RACHEL
HANCOCK

A QUICK-REFERENCE GUIDE TO
75 Healing Stones

FAIR WINDS

CONTENTS

CHAPTER 1

WHERE DO YOU BEGIN? 7
crystal basics and how to use them

CHAPTER 2

GET TO KNOW 75 CRYSTALS 21
a crystal directory

index of crystals 172

acknowledgments 174

about the author 176

WHERE DO YOU BEGIN?

crystal basics and how to use them

WHEN YOU START YOUR CRYSTAL HEALING journey, deciding which crystals to use to aid specific aspects of your life, mind, or body can be overwhelming. Start off slow and steady, so you can care for, love, and understand the energy of each of your crystals and its impact on your overall well-being.

CHOOSING A CRYSTAL

Shopping for crystals is exciting yet overwhelming. Using your intuition is the best way to decide which crystal is best for you. Make sure to ground yourself first by taking a short walk outside barefoot, doing a 10-minute meditation, or closing your eyes and gently tapping your thymus for 20 to 30 seconds.

While shopping, be aware of which crystal really draws you in. It may be a certain color, shape, or type of crystal. This awareness will give you a greater understanding of which crystal(s) to choose. Set the crystals that you're drawn to out in front of you. Quickly and firmly rub your palms together for 20 to 30 seconds, or until you feel a sense of heat rising. Slowly hover your nondominant hand over each crystal, with your palm facing the crystal. As you scan each crystal, ask your intuition to tell you whether the crystal is right for you. You may feel heat, a tingly sensation, a loud yes from the universe, or another message from your intuition.

If shopping online, ask your intuition to tell you whether each crystal is right for you. If the online listing is one where you cannot individually select your crystal and you want to be pickier, try messaging the seller to see if they can show you options.

CLEANSING A CRYSTAL

Ensure that your crystal is free of any stored-up energy residue before using it. Crystals absorb all energy, good and bad, so they may take on energy from a previous owner, a crystal shop, or their travels. How often you need to cleanse your crystal after the first use depends on how often you will be working with it and for how long. You can tell a crystal needs to be cleansed when:

- The energy feels dull, empty, or lifeless.

- You or a loved one just used it.

- It seems less effective when you are using it.

The following are a few ways to cleanse your crystals. First, though, consult the precautions in the Crystal Directory in this book. Some crystals should not be put in direct sunlight or in water.

Sunlight
Place your crystal(s) out in direct sunlight for 1 to 2 hours.

Moonlight
Place your crystal(s) out in direct moonlight overnight. Check below for specific cleansing intentions depending on which phase the moon is in. If you live in a place where you cannot take your crystals into direct moonlight, place them on your windowsill.

Water
Place your crystal(s) in a bowl of water from a natural body of water (such as a lake, river, or ocean) or lightly sea-salted water. Keep them in the bowl for 1 to 5 minutes and then rinse them with regular tap water. Leave them out to air-dry.

Sound Vibration

Sound waves pass through the crystal and release energy stored within it. Place your crystal next to a sound vibrational tool, such as a sound bowl, tingsha, bell, tuning fork, gong, or crystal pyramid. Play the instrument for a couple of minutes.

Selenite or Clear Quartz

Place your crystal(s) on a selenite or clear quartz plate or bowl. Leave them to cleanse for at least 4 to 6 hours.

Energetic Intentional Breath

For this method, you can use Reiki or intentional visualization. Place the crystal in your hand. As you breathe in, visualize your hand filling up with pure bright light and expanding that light into the crystal. As you breathe out, visualize any stagnant, negative, or stuck energy releasing from the crystal. Continue this breathing technique until you intuitively feel the crystal has been cleansed.

Sage, Palo Santo, or Incense

Light your sage, palo santo, or incense and pass the crystal(s) through the smoke for 30 seconds to a few minutes. One way you will know whether the clearing work is done is that the smoke will move to one side of the crystal instead of all over.

CHARGING A CRYSTAL

Charging helps the crystal operate at its highest vibration. How often you need to charge your crystal after the first use depends on how often you will be working with it and for how long.

Here are a few good ways to charge your crystals.

Sunlight
Place your crystal(s) out in direct sunlight for 1 to 2 hours.

Moonlight
Place your crystal(s) out in direct moonlight overnight.

Copper Pyramids
Copper pyramids represent enhanced energy, preservation, purification, protection, and spiritual connection. Place your crystal(s) in the center of your pyramid for at least 6 hours. Keep a pyramid near your bedside for a nightly charging station.

Sound Vibration
Sound waves pass through the crystal, restore its energy, and put it back into balance. Place your crystal next to a sound vibrational tool, such as a sound bowl, tingsha, bell, tuning fork, gong, or crystal pyramid. Play the instrument for a couple of minutes.

Selenite or Clear Quartz
Place your crystal(s) on a selenite or clear quartz plate or bowl. You can charge your crystal(s) by your bedside overnight or leave them to charge throughout the day. I recommend leaving it to charge for at least 4 to 6 hours. This process can be done simultaneously with the cleansing process.

Clear Quartz Grid

Place six clear quartz points around your crystal, facing inward toward it. I recommend leaving it to charge for at least 4 to 6 hours.

Dried Herbs, Seeds, Leaves, or Flowers

Place your crystal in a bowl and fill the bowl with your choice of dried herbs, seeds, leaves, flowers, or even a combination of them all. Make sure the crystal is completely covered and leave it overnight to charge.

Snow

Place your crystal outside and completely cover it with snow. Make sure you mark the place you have chosen so it doesn't get lost. Leave it overnight to charge. Snow brings the intentions of peace and serenity to the crystal.

Storm

Place your crystal outside during a storm, somewhere it has direct connection to mother nature. I recommend leaving it to charge for at least 2 to 3 hours. Storms bring the intentions of excitement, renewal, and balance to the crystal.

Fog

Place your crystal outside in the fog, preferably where it has direct connection to mother nature. I recommend leaving it to charge overnight. Fog brings the intentions of protection and overcoming obstacles to the crystal.

MOON PHASES & THEIR CLEANSING AND CHARGING INTENTIONS

Different phases of the moon bring different intentions to your cleansing and charging.

- **New moon:** new beginnings, clear intentions, new opportunities, self-reflection, self-care, and renewal

- **Waxing crescent:** planning, preparing, positive energy, amplified manifestations, inner wisdom, personal strength, optimism, and communication

- **First quarter:** supporting intentions, love and romance, determination, commitment, overall health and wellness, and courage

- **Waxing gibbous:** moving forward, cultivating intentions, taking action, acceptance, surrender, creativity, tranquility, and commitment

- **Full moon:** amplified intentions, abundance, manifestation, heightened intuition, transformation, personal power, protection, and flow

- **Waning gibbous:** letting go of what doesn't serve you, setting boundaries, gratitude, nurturing, and reflection

- **Last quarter:** compassion, release, enjoying accomplishments, independence, success, blossoming, and epiphany

- **Waning crescent:** solitude, relaxation, rest, solidification, preparation for new intentions to be set, stillness, release, and reflection

ATTUNING TO A CRYSTAL'S ENERGY

When you first come in contact with your crystal, you naturally begin to attune to its energy, which causes subtle changes in your energy field. By tuning into your crystal's energy, you will be able to raise your vibrations and understand your crystal on a deeper level.

Begin by grounding and centering yourself. You can do this by closing your eyes and gently tapping your thymus for 20 to 30 seconds or by doing a 3-minute meditation. Then quickly and firmly rub your palms together for 20 to 30 seconds or until you feel heat rising. Pick up your crystal and become aware of its energy. How does it feel to touch? How does it feel when it's on your body? How does it make you feel?

You may want to keep a crystal journal next to you so you can take note of your crystal's energy. You may come to find that it's not the right time just yet to be working with it—or that it's exactly what you need in your life at this time. By understanding your crystal's energy, you will be able to be more intuitively guided as to when to use and not use it, when it needs to be cleansed or charged, and how it's affecting your energy and overall well-being.

SET INTENTIONS

Each crystal's unique structure is believed to store energy, ideas, and memories. And each crystal has multiple healing properties, so by setting your intentions before using it, you can program it to work for a specific healing, goal, or intention. You are simultaneously programming yourself by focusing on exactly what you want to heal or achieve. To set your intentions, hold your crystal up to your third-eye chakra level with both hands, close your eyes, and focus on the crystal. As you do, envision your intention and repeat the affirmation, "Crystal, please assist me with __." Fill in the blank with your specific intention. Repeat this affirmation several times until you feel that the crystal's energy is programmed. This should make you feel good and warm.

PLACE CRYSTALS WITH INTENTION

Finally, intentionally place your crystal somewhere in your home, in a crystal layout on your body (skin contact is preferable for better results), somewhere it will be taken with you, or on a crystal grid.

HIGH VIBRATIONAL VERSUS SOOTHING VIBRATIONAL CRYSTALS

Some crystals are gentler and others have a very high vibrational pull. This topic is especially important for sensitive souls and empaths—as a beginner, you should start off with a gentler and more soothing crystal, so you don't feel overwhelmed and overworked and possibly withdraw from crystals because it feels too much for you.

For example, moldavite, one of the highest vibrational tektites, is so high vibration that almost anyone can feel its energy, no matter how sensitive they are. And it shouldn't be taken lightly. It's known for giving people a "moldavite flush"—a huge opening of the heart chakra that can cause a flush in the face, anxiety, lightheadedness, dizziness, an overwhelming sensation of emotional release, and even the feeling of being lifted out of your body. This is because moldavite and other high vibrational crystals excite and speed up your vibrations at a rapid pace.

Your body needs to become acclimated to these high vibrations. To acclimate, slowly introduce your body to a crystal's vibrations. Start with 1 minute and see how its energy feels for you. Then up it to 2 to 3 minutes the next day or whenever you're ready. It took me three weeks to be able to meditate with moldavite for 10 minutes, but some people can wear it all day immediately. This is why attuning to its energy is such an important step when getting your crystal. Please listen to your body, but don't be afraid to get uncomfortable. Change doesn't come from comfort. We want to release what no longer serves our best selves—but only through love and care.

CRYSTAL PRECAUTIONS

Here are some safety concerns to keep in mind. See chapter 2 for crystal-specific precautions.

- Not all crystals are safe to put in water, and some contain toxic or hazardous minerals that shouldn't be ingested.

- Do not push the process and overwhelm your system with too many crystals at once. Honor your intuition. If you are having negative side effects, completely stop using your crystals for a time.

- Not all crystals are safe to put outside in the sunlight for a prolonged period. Some can crack, break, fade, or even start a fire! Some of the most photosensitive crystals are beryls, quartz, and calcites. You can always place any crystal outside for 5 to 10 minutes, but if you're unsure, don't go any longer than that.

- Not all crystals have a soft gentle energy. You don't want to be overwhelmed, overworked, or possibly convinced to withdraw from crystals because the energy is too much for you. Listen to your intuition.

- Crystals that amplify energy, such as clear quartz, can bring in positive energy and remove negative energy from the body if placed correctly. However, it can also amplify or exacerbate physical symptoms if not used correctly.

OH NO, MY CRYSTAL BROKE! NOW WHAT?

Throughout your crystal journey, you may break a crystal or two. If you crack, break, or chip a crystal, it does not lose its healing properties, but there are a couple of spiritual meanings behind a broken crystal. One is that the crystal has done its work. When it breaks, it's letting you know that it's time to move on from that crystal. And if it's a protective crystal such as amethyst, black obsidian, or black tourmaline, it could have broken while protecting you from intense negative energy. Regardless of the meaning, it's up to you to decide what to do with it next. Let your intuition guide you as to whether you glue it back together, cleanse and charge it, gift it, or do anything else that best serves you.

STORING CRYSTALS

Ultimately you want to use your inner guidance when choosing where you want to display crystals in your home. However, some important considerations when storing your crystals are:

- Is the crystal okay in prolonged sun exposure? If it's not, you will want to avoid putting it in direct sunlight from your windowsill or outside in your garden.

- Is your crystal soft? If it's a 5 or below on the Mohs scale of mineral hardness, I would make sure it isn't touching any other crystals, so it doesn't scratch and is in a safe place where it cannot fall. If it does, it will more than likely chip or break.

- If you choose to put your crystal in a container, make sure that it won't damage it. The safest containers are made of wood, cotton, silk, or anything soft to the touch.

- Keep your most precious crystals in a safe place where they won't be touched by others.

get to know 75 crystals

A CRYSTAL DIRECTORY

RED JASPER

Grounding · Strength · Energy · Fulfillment
Mental Stability

COLOR	red
CHAKRA	root
ZODIAC SIGNS	Leo, Virgo, Scorpio, and Taurus
ELEMENT	earth
CRYSTAL PAIRINGS	agate, garnet, petrified wood, smoky quartz, or sardonyx
PRECAUTIONS	none
AFFIRMATION	I am rooted into the earth like a tree— grounded, safe, and secure

Spiritual Healing

- Deepens your meditation and raises your Kundalini energy.
- Assists you in setting boundaries.
- Gives you a sense of stability, safety, security, and grounding.
- Increases your life force (prana).
- Provides a protective energy shield from negative energy and danger.

Physical Healing

- Can help replenish your muscles after a workout.
- Boosts physical energy, stamina, vitality, and strength.
- Aids in speeding up recovery after an illness or surgery.
- Can detoxify the liver, circulatory system, and bile ducts.
- Supports a healthy heart.

Emotional Healing

- Helps you maintain your mental stability.
- Works to release feelings of irritability, guilt, shame, or regret.
- Helps soothe upset feelings and calm your emotions.
- Helps bring more joy to your life by letting you become more present in the moment.
- Increases willpower and mental strength.

GARNET

Strength · Love · Joy · Life Force · Power

COLOR	deep red, orange, brown, yellow, pink, green, and blue
CHAKRA	root and heart
ZODIAC SIGNS	Aquarius, Capricorn, Aries, Leo, and Virgo
ELEMENT	earth and fire
CRYSTAL PAIRINGS	serpentine, vanadanite, ruby, or red jasper
PRECAUTIONS	Garnet contains aluminum and can be toxic if ingested. Avoid putting it in direct sunlight, as its color will begin to fade.
AFFIRMATION	I am living my life with purpose, love, and passion.

Spiritual Healing

- Works on releasing karmic contracts.

- Enhances and deepens your meditation.

- Increases Kundalini life force energy.

- Provides an energetic shield of protection from negativity.

- Increases feeling grounded into mother nature's healing energy.

Physical Healing

- Boosts fertility, passion, motivation, libido, and sensuality.

- Supports a healthy heart, lungs, and blood.

- Helps speed up the recovery process after surgery or an injury.

- Revitalizes, strengthens, and rejuvenates the physical body.

Emotional Healing

- Can help you overcome anxiety, stress, worry, and fear.

- Helps relieve depression, chaos, and emotional trauma.

- Enhances understanding, trust, expression, and honesty with yourself and others.

- Encourages change, creativity, abundance, courage, and awareness.

- Can help with emotional stability and increasing one's ability to feel love.

- Brings feelings of warmth, love, nourishment, and romance.

SUNSTONE

Abundance · Joy · Creativity · Strength · Energy

COLOR	orange
CHAKRA	all, especially sacral
ZODIAC SIGNS	Leo and Libra
ELEMENT	fire
CRYSTAL PAIRINGS	iolite, labradorite, or ocean jasper
PRECAUTIONS	Do not allow prolonged sun exposure.
AFFIRMATION	I am in charge of how I feel today, and today I choose joy.

Spiritual Healing

- Brings positive energy and abundance.
- Can aid in protection against negativity and evil spirits.
- Clears and energizes all seven chakras.
- Encourages you to be your most authentic self.
- Sparks new ideas, creativity, and visions.

Physical Healing

- Aids in improving overall health and well-being.
- Stimulates sexuality, passion, and libido.
- Assists in vitality, strength, energy, and longevity.
- Supports a healthy circulatory and nervous system.

Emotional Healing

- Can help relieve stress and conquer fears.
- Boosts feelings of optimism, euphoria, and self-care.
- Helps individuals battling depression find happiness and joy again.
- Encourages independence and originality.
- Boosts feelings of self-confidence, courage, and self-worth.
- Encourages healthy and positive relationships.

CARNELIAN

Creativity · Vitality · Energy · Confidence · Sensuality

COLOR	red, orange, yellow, and white
CHAKRA	sacral
ZODIAC SIGNS	Virgo, Taurus, Cancer, and Leo
ELEMENT	fire
CRYSTAL PAIRINGS	citrine, rose quartz, red garnet, sardonyx, or shiva lingam
PRECAUTIONS	Carnelian is not safe in salt water.
AFFIRMATION	I have the energy and stamina to achieve anything I desire.

Spiritual Healing

- Boosts your ability to manifest your dreams and desires.
- Sparks creativity and imagination.
- Provides an energetic protection from negative and toxic energy.
- Boosts an abundance of love, positive energy, and light in your life.
- Can clear out negative energy from other crystals.

Physical Healing

- Boosts sex drive and fertility.
- Helps promote blood circulation and purification.
- Boosts energy, passion, stamina, motivation, and vitality.
- Provides peace during menstrual and menopausal symptoms.
- Supports a healthy immune system and reproductive system.

Emotional Healing

- Increases enthusiasm and optimism for enjoying everything life has to offer.
- Aids in the treatment of eating disorders and disordered thinking.
- Helps you set boundaries with others.
- Increases feelings of self-confidence and self-worth.
- Encourages healthy relationships with your partner, loved ones, and friendships.

SARDONYX

Loving Relationships • Security • Happiness
Energy • Creativity

COLOR	orange, red, yellow, and black
CHAKRA	sacral
ZODIAC SIGNS	Virgo
ELEMENT	fire
CRYSTAL PAIRINGS	carnelian or red jasper
PRECAUTIONS	none
AFFIRMATION	I attract happiness, security, and loving relationships.

Spiritual Healing

- Promotes energetic grounding and protection.
- Enhances your creativity, sparking new ideas and explorations.
- Urges you to strive for a fulfilling life.
- Is a stone of courage, good luck, and strength.

Physical Healing

- Boosts endurance, passion, vitality, and energy.
- Brings the metabolism back into balance.
- Helps maintain a healthy immune system.
- Supports healthy lungs and bones.

Emotional Healing

- Helps with lasting happiness and clear communication.
- Brings in feelings of positivity, optimism, and happiness.
- Can aid in eliminating hesitations.
- Aids in positive socializing, marriage, and relationships with others.
- Boosts feelings of joy and gratitude, helping one overcome depression.
- Enhances confidence and honesty within yourself.
- Promotes feelings of safety and security.

CITRINE

Abundance · Joy · Digestive Balance · Wealth · Luck

COLOR	yellow
CHAKRA	solar plexus
ZODIAC SIGNS	Cancer
ELEMENT	fire
CRYSTAL PAIRINGS	carnelian, pyrite, moldavite, Libyan desert glass, golden healer, honey calcite, opal, or peridot
PRECAUTIONS	Citrine's color will fade in direct sunlight.
AFFIRMATION	I radiate joy and confidence in every cell of my being.

Spiritual Healing

- Radiates high vibrational energy, making it perfect when manifesting prosperity, success, and abundance.

- Guides us to find our soul purpose in this lifetime.

- Stimulates a deeper connection with your higher self and spirit guides.

- Promotes new perceptions, creativity, and ideas.

- Opens, activates, and balances the solar plexus chakra.

Physical Healing

- Helps bring balance and healing to the digestive system and metabolism.

- Is known to boost stamina, endurance, and physical energy.

- Works to regulate a healthy liver and kidneys.

- Helps support and balance the endocrine system and hormones.

- Supports healthy blood flow and circulation.

Emotional Healing

- Helps reduce fear, worry, and anxiety.

- Aids in stimulating mental focus, personal empowerment, productivity, and mental clarity.

- Can strengthen self-confidence, personal power, and self-esteem.

- Helps you develop a positive attitude toward anything that life swings at you.

- Provides support in releasing old limiting beliefs.

GOLDEN HEALER

Abundance • Golden Light • Confidence
Happiness • Empathy

COLOR	yellow and white
CHAKRA	solar plexus
ZODIAC SIGNS	Leo
ELEMENT	water and air
CRYSTAL PAIRINGS	citrine, honey calcite, lemurian, Libyan desert glass, or ocean jasper
PRECAUTIONS	Do not keep golden healer in direct sunlight, as the color will begin to fade.
AFFIRMATION	I am constantly attracting positivity and abundance into my life.

Spiritual Healing

- Harmonizes your yin and yang energies.
- Helps raise your vibrations.
- Connects and awakens you to the healing universal golden light.
- Works on clearing energetic blockages and restoring your body back into balance.
- Connects you to your higher self and personal power.

Physical Healing

- Enhances physical vitality and energy.
- Helps you make large life changes with little effort.
- Aids in cleansing and restoring all organs in the body.
- Boosts feelings of happiness and joy to bring health and abundance into the home.
- Supports a healthy digestive system.

Emotional Healing

- Brings feelings of joy, empathy, compassion, happiness, and love.
- Calms the mind, bringing a sense of peace and harmony.
- Boosts feelings of self-worth, self-confidence, and self-love.
- Helps heal old emotional wounds and release what no longer serves you.
- Encourages you to move forward after going through a negative experience.

LIBYAN DESERT GLASS

Manifestation · Confidence · Joy · Abundance
Highly Vibrational

COLOR	yellow
CHAKRA	all, especially solar plexus
ZODIAC SIGNS	Virgo and Gemini
ELEMENT	fire and storm
CRYSTAL PAIRINGS	moldavite, citrine, golden healer, honey calcite, herkimer diamond, prehnite, or serpentine
PRECAUTIONS	none
AFFIRMATION	I am divinely guided to manifest for my highest good.

Spiritual Healing

- Speeds up manifestations and self-transformation.
- Awakens the king or queen energy within you.
- Helps you find your soul purpose in life.
- Is highly vibrational and can even take you to other realms.
- Connects and awakens you to the healing universal golden light.
- Sparks and enhances your creativity and new ideas.

Physical Healing

- Can provide relief for any imbalances in the digestive tract.
- Helps support and balance the immune and endocrine systems.
- Brings balance to any physical symptoms that arise from stress.
- Provides a renewal of your physical vitality.

Emotional Healing

- Helps you set boundaries to form the ultimate love for yourself.
- Boosts inner feelings of joy, playfulness, and adequacy.
- Enables you to claim and strengthen your personal power.
- Boosts self-confidence to help you come out of your shell.
- Instills sympathy, filling your mind with kind, gentle, and understanding thoughts about others.

HONEY CALCITE

Joy · Confidence · Courage · Angels · Purpose

COLOR	yellow and orange
CHAKRA	solar plexus
ZODIAC SIGNS	Cancer, Leo, Pisces, and Aries
ELEMENT	fire and wind
CRYSTAL PAIRINGS	golden healer, celestite, herkimer diamond, citrine, Libyan desert glass, or septarian
PRECAUTIONS	Do not put honey calcite in water, because it is a very soft, brittle stone. Do not put it in prolonged direct sunlight; it can become brittle and break.
AFFIRMATION	I am constantly beaming universal golden light that surrounds and protects me.

Spiritual Healing

- Attunes you to higher angelic realms and consciousness.

- Cleanses and purifies your home's energy.

- Helps you strengthen your manifestations to achieve your higher purpose in life.

- Increases physical, mental, and spiritual energetic growth.

- Provides spiritual guidance in achieving your goals.

Physical Healing

- Promotes healthy blood sugar levels, endocrine function, and digestion.

- Encourages children's healthy development.

- Reduces inflammation.

- Helps detoxify the kidney, bladder, and bowels.

Emotional Healing

- Allows you to be more open-minded and embrace change with open arms.

- Brings feelings of joy, hope, and optimism.

- Allows you to let go of what no longer serves you.

- Works to increase your feelings of self-worth, inner strength, confidence, and courage.

- Can show you how to recognize and use your personal power.

- Helps you get back on your feet after being knocked down by a challenging situation.

SEPTARIAN

Grounding · Nurturing · Courage
Confidence · Transformation

COLOR	yellow and brown
CHAKRA	root, sacral, and solar plexus
ZODIAC SIGNS	Taurus, Leo, Virgo, Capricorn, and Scorpio
ELEMENT	fire
CRYSTAL PAIRINGS	honey calcite or tiger's eye
PRECAUTIONS	Septarian is a soft stone; do not put it in water.
AFFIRMATION	I am grounded, safe, and protected at all times.

Spiritual Healing

- Is a nurturing, protective, and grounding stone.
- Enhances your dreams and provides a vividness one has yet to experience.
- Harmonizes our inner and outer selves.
- Helps you dive into transformation by going deep within.
- Aids in restoring and regulating blocked energies in the solar plexus.

Physical Healing

- Can help calm an upset stomach or any imbalance in the digestive system.
- Aids in strengthening the bones, teeth, and muscles.
- Supports healthy blood and kidneys.
- Promotes overall good health and well-being.

Emotional Healing

- Helps you keep your focus on one project at a time.
- Promotes courage, personal power, and bravery.
- Helps you get through extreme life changes by balancing and repairing your emotional body.
- Boosts feelings of joy, confidence, self-esteem, and gratitude.
- Helps you become more patient with others.
- Can help release emotional stress, anxiety, or depression.

AMBER

Joy · Purification · Radiance · Warmth · Healing

COLOR	yellow, gold, and honey
CHAKRA	solar plexus
ZODIAC SIGNS	Leo and Scorpio
ELEMENT	earth
CRYSTAL PAIRINGS	lemurian or jet
PRECAUTIONS	Do not place amber in water; it is too soft.
AFFIRMATION	I have the willpower to set boundaries with love and grace, which allows me to be protected from negative energy.

Spiritual Healing

- Helps you find your soul purpose in life.
- Aids in speeding up and amplifying your manifestations.
- Helps purify, protect, and expand your auric field.
- Can clear out all karmic debris and past-life traumas.
- Helps you connect to your higher consciousness and awareness.

Physical Healing

- Is said to absorb and remove pain from the body.
- Helps boost energy levels, longevity, and vitality.
- Connects us to the core of our overall well-being.
- Helps in maintaining a healthy immune system.
- Aids in reducing inflammation and swelling in the body.

Emotional Healing

- Boosts self-confidence and self-expression.
- Brings wisdom, balance, and patience.
- Boosts feelings of joy and gratitude, helping one overcome depression.
- Helps banish all fears so you can see life in an abundance of joy, radiance, and love.
- Promotes releasing and healing emotional traumas.

NEPHRITE GREEN JADE

Good Luck · Grounding · Protection · Health
Heart Healing

COLOR	green
CHAKRA	root and heart
ZODIAC SIGNS	Virgo, Pisces, and Taurus
ELEMENT	earth
CRYSTAL PAIRINGS	epidote, green aventurine, pyrite, moss agate, serpentine, or shungite
PRECAUTIONS	Do not leave nephrite jade out in prolonged sunlight; its color may begin to fade.
AFFIRMATION	My body is constantly attracting what's best for me.

Spiritual Healing

- Brings good luck, protection, and fortune.
- Is an earth-healing stone that connects us with mother nature as one.
- Is known to change your negative energy into positive energy.
- Stimulates lucid and vivid dreaming.
- Brings balance to your feminine and masculine energies.
- Frees you from your karmic cycle.

Physical Healing

- Brings strength and health to the physical body.
- Helps heal all imbalances in the metabolism, skin, hair, kidneys, and adrenals.
- Aids in bringing the nervous system back into harmony.
- Helps strengthen the heart.
- Promotes a peaceful night's rest.

Emotional Healing

- Promotes happy and healthy relationships.
- Instills feelings of nostalgia, peace, harmony, and hope.
- Allows you to open your heart to love others at a deep level.
- Stimulates the release of limiting beliefs.

MALACHITE

Emotional Release · Heart Healing
Highly Vibrational · Transformation · Love

COLOR	green
CHAKRA	heart
ZODIAC SIGNS	Taurus, Virgo, Capricorn, and Scorpio
ELEMENT	earth, water, and fire
CRYSTAL PAIRINGS	azurite, chrysocolla, tiger's eye, turquoise, or morganite
PRECAUTIONS	Do not place malachite in water; it contains copper and is a soft stone. Do not place it in direct sunlight, because the color will begin to fade.
AFFIRMATION	I let go of old emotional baggage that no longer serves me.

Spiritual Healing

- Clears, activates, and balances all the chakras, especially the heart chakra.

- Increases positive light and vibrations for the auric field.

- Supports inner and creative visualizations.

- Is a stone of transformation, assisting you through big changes in your life.

- Helps you move beyond your ego to altruism.

- Enhances spirituality and psychic abilities.

Physical Healing

- Can align and cleanse cellular and DNA structures.

- Works to restore and increase physical strength and vitality.

- Can provide protection from all types of radiation.

- Supports a healthy immune system.

- Aids in the treatment of broken bones, swollen joints, asthma, and arthritis.

Emotional Healing

- Increases unconditional love for yourself and others.

- Helps heal old emotional abuse and wounds, especially from childhood trauma.

- Aids in releasing repressed emotions stored in the subconscious mind.

- Encourages healthy relationships based on love and compassion.

BLOODSTONE

Flow · Release · Purification · Courage · Grounding

COLOR	green and red
CHAKRA	root, sacral, and heart
ZODIAC SIGNS	Aries, Pisces, and Libra
ELEMENT	earth
CRYSTAL PAIRINGS	black tourmaline, jet, black obsidian, or lemurian
PRECAUTIONS	Do not submerge bloodstone in water; it can rust.
AFFIRMATION	I am strong, courageous, and brave enough to conquer anything.

Spiritual Healing

- Is grounding, reconnecting you to the earth's energy.
- Helps you live more present in the moment.
- Has been known and used for centuries to banish evil and dispel negativity.
- Expands and heightens your intuition.
- Opens and awakens communication with spiritual realms.

Physical Healing

- Can aid in your recovery from an illness, surgery, or injury.
- Helps bring your hormones back into a healthy and balanced state.
- Supports healthy blood flow and circulation.
- Helps detoxify and purify the physical body, especially the blood.
- Supports nutrient absorption.

Emotional Healing

- Calms the mind and increases your ability to make rational decisions.
- Aids in releasing emotional stress, temper, and aggression.
- Promotes calmness and emotional centering.
- Encourages selflessness, idealism, kindness, and generosity.
- Is a stone of courage, promoting strength to face your fears.

EMERALD

Heart Healing · Love · Compassion · Empathy · Kindness

COLOR	green
CHAKRA	heart
ZODIAC SIGNS	Taurus, Capricorn, and Virgo
ELEMENT	earth and water
CRYSTAL PAIRINGS	rose quartz, kunzite, rhodochrosite, green aventurine, morganite, prehnite, or serpentine
PRECAUTIONS	Emerald contains aluminum and can be toxic if ingested. Direct sunlight should also be avoided; its color will fade.
AFFIRMATION	When I open my heart up to love, I am filled with an abundance of love and light.

Spiritual Healing

- Helps you develop trust with the universe that everything happens in divine timing.

- Can enhance psychic abilities.

- Stimulates your ability to receive fortune and abundance.

- Bathes the auric field in an abundance of green healing light.

- Works to cleanse the energetic body of any karmic contracts.

Physical Healing

- Helps heal the heart from a heartbreak, physical imbalances of the heart, or heart diseases.

- Can lessen symptoms that stem from diabetes.

- Aids in relieving joint pain.

- Helps in recovering after an infection.

- Is known as a master physical healer, providing overall health and wellness.

Emotional Healing

- Helps attract or keep positive relationships with others.

- Opens the heart to feeling unconditional love for yourself and others.

- Stimulates empathy, sympathy, and kindness.

- Helps you overcome fears of abandonment, unworthiness, and loneliness.

- Is a nourishing stone, promoting forgiveness and compassion.

GREEN AVENTURINE

Optimism · Luck · Abundance · Emotional Well-Being · Vitality

COLOR	green
CHAKRA	heart
ZODIAC SIGNS	Taurus, Virgo, Capricorn, and Libra
ELEMENT	earth and water
CRYSTAL PAIRINGS	rose quartz, emerald, nephrite jade, prehnite, morganite, or pyrite
PRECAUTIONS	Avoid putting green aventurine in direct sunlight; the color will begin to fade.
AFFIRMATION	I am a magnet for abundance.

Spiritual Healing

- Magnifies your ability to manifest good luck and fortune.
- Encourages spiritual growth and development.
- Allows you to attract and receive abundance into your life.
- Releases negative attachments to other things, allowing you to reconnect with what matters.
- Energetically provides a shield of protection for your home and garden.

Physical Healing

- Boosts physical energy and vitality.
- Can help strengthen the muscles, lungs, and heart.
- Aids in improving overall health and well-being.
- Can reduce clumsiness by assisting with your center of gravity.
- Aids in detoxifying and cleansing the organs.

Emotional Healing

- Helps improve decision-making and leadership abilities.
- Aids in removing aggression, negative thoughts, and irritability.
- Promotes relaxation and emotional well-being.
- Helps you feel optimistic and motivated again.
- Encourages self-love and self-care.

GARNIERITE

Emotional Stability · Unconditional Love
Well-Being · Kindness · Confidence

COLOR	green, blue, and gray
CHAKRA	heart
ZODIAC SIGNS	Leo and Virgo
ELEMENT	water
CRYSTAL PAIRINGS	rainbow moonstone, rose quartz, morganite, kunzite, or turquoise
PRECAUTIONS	Garnierite contains aluminum and can be toxic if ingested. It is a soft stone; do not put it in water. Avoid putting it in direct sunlight, as its color will begin to fade.
AFFIRMATION	I love my mind. I love my body. I love my spirit.

Spiritual Healing

- Works to balance your feminine energy.
- Helps you move beyond your ego to altruism.
- Helps you set boundaries.
- Works as a companion during your spiritual growth and development.
- Fills you up with unconditional love and light.

Physical Healing

- Provides an energy boost to get you through your day.
- Encourages a sense of overall health and well-being.
- Aids in strengthening the heart, lungs, and muscles.
- Helps if you struggle with being sensitive to sound.
- Increases strength, motivation, and perseverance.

Emotional Healing

- Guides you on how to fully love yourself and others unconditionally.
- Helps you conquer your fears in order to achieve and manifest your dreams.
- Helps bring your emotions into balance and stability.
- Increases feelings of self-confidence and self-worth.
- Brings mental clarity when seeking the truth.

MOSS AGATE

Earthiness · New Beginnings · Abundance
Balance · Stability

COLOR	green and white
CHAKRA	root and heart
ZODIAC SIGNS	Capricorn, Virgo, and Taurus
ELEMENT	earth
CRYSTAL PAIRINGS	fluorite, epidote, petrified wood, or nephrite jade
PRECAUTIONS	Never clean moss agate with household chemicals or leave it out in direct sunlight for hours because most moss agate contains quartz.
AFFIRMATION	I am nourished by mother nature and life itself.

Spiritual Healing

- Helps you go through change and new beginnings with ease and excitement.

- Helps you create and find your purpose in life.

- Facilitates connection to mother nature, helping you become more present and grounded in the physical world.

- Brings positive energy and abundance.

- Helps speed up the manifestation process.

Physical Healing

- Acts as an anti-inflammatory, helping treat skin and fungal infections.

- Brings the body back into alignment and balance.

- Stimulates the brain and memory functions.

- Helps heal the physical body.

- Supports a healthy immune system.

Emotional Healing

- Helps you release old, negative patterns and fears.

- Can relieve anxiety, stress, and worry.

- Brings in new friendships with like-minded energy and beliefs.

- Enhances mental stability, concentration, stamina, and completion.

- Helps balance the emotions, preventing irrational mood swings.

MOLDAVITE

Manifestation · Trauma Healing · Highly Vibrational
Transformational · Raises Vibrations

COLOR	green
CHAKRA	heart, third eye, and crown
ZODIAC SIGNS	all
ELEMENT	storm
CRYSTAL PAIRINGS	charoite, citrine, herkimer diamond, Libyan desert glass, black tourmaline, lemurian, or rainbow moonstone
PRECAUTIONS	Gradually adjust yourself to moldavite's high frequency. Start by wearing or using it for a minute at a time. It may take days or weeks until you're ready to use it for a full meditation or day.
AFFIRMATION	I welcome an abundant mindset.

Spiritual Healing

- Awakens and balances your Kundalini energy.
- Connects you to higher spirit realms, your higher self, spirit guides, other dimensions, and extraterrestrials.
- Magnifies and speeds up the process of transformation and manifestations.
- Enhances your dream state; it is great for lucid dreaming and astral travel.
- Is extremely powerful and known to create an energetic flush.
- Is an extremely high vibrational tektite.
- Stimulates your intuition and psychic abilities.
- Assists in deepening your meditation and connecting to your higher consciousness.

Physical Healing

- Can provide relief from asthma, allergies, or rashes.
- Is only to be used if you are ready to bring up the root causes of your imbalances or illnesses, because it will create a "healing crisis."
- Awakens the presence of trapped emotions and spiritual wounds and brings them to the surface for them to be healed.

Emotional Healing

- Radiates love and opening of the heart.
- Helps remove irrational fears and doubts.
- Boosts feelings of personal power and will.
- Initiates creativity so you can make better decisions.

PERIDOT

Love · Prosperity · Health · Joy · Animal Communication

COLOR	green
CHAKRA	solar plexus and heart
ZODIAC SIGNS	Leo, Virgo, and Taurus
ELEMENT	earth and air
CRYSTAL PAIRINGS	herkimer diamond, morganite, prehnite, ruby, or citrine
PRECAUTIONS	none
AFFIRMATION	I am a magnet for abundance.

Spiritual Healing

- Helps remove deep blockages located in the back of the chakras.

- Aids in animal communication and healing.

- Assists in protection from negative energy and evil spirits.

- Manifests spiritual abundance, success, and luck.

- Invites spiritual wisdom and connection.

Physical Healing

- Helps heal the heart, physically and emotionally.

- Aids in strengthening and promoting a healthy blood flow.

- Helps support and balance the endocrine system.

- Rejuvenates energy in the physical body.

- Promotes a healthy liver, gallbladder, spleen, intestines, heart, and lungs.

Emotional Healing

- Helps you manifest prosperity, health, and joy in abundance.

- Helps you recover from your addictions.

- Opens your heart to receiving love, grace, and gratitude.

- Builds your confidence and feelings of self-worth.

- Helps release built-up anger, tension, or jealousy.

SERPENTINE

Kundalini Energy Awakening · Compassion
Love · Purification · Connection

COLOR	green
CHAKRA	all, especially heart
ZODIAC SIGNS	Gemini, Scorpio, Taurus, Virgo, and Capricorn
ELEMENT	earth
CRYSTAL PAIRINGS	nephrite jade, Libyan desert glass, tiger's eye, emerald, or jet
PRECAUTIONS	Avoid cleansing serpentine in water; most serpentine is softer, so it can become brittle and crack with water.
AFFIRMATION	Today I will be mindful, happy, and live in the moment.

Spiritual Healing

- Awakens and balances your Kundalini energy.
- Helps clear any blocked energies and then allows a natural healthy flow of energy to go through.
- Enhances animal, mother nature, and spiritual connections.
- Provides an energetic protection field in your aura so you don't have other toxic energies seep into yours.
- Is grounding, reconnecting you to the earth's healing energy.

Physical Healing

- Helps in cellular regeneration and in replenishing your energy.
- Supports a healthy digestive system.
- Promotes a healthy heart, kidneys, and skin.
- Helps improve circulation and purification of the blood.
- Helps rejuvenate the body's tissues.
- Aids in the treatment of diabetes or hypoglycemia symptoms.

Emotional Healing

- Allows you to release your fears of change and any fearful ideas of your future.
- Opens your heart to giving to others from the goodness of your heart.
- Promotes feelings of love, compassion, and forgiveness.
- Works to balance and stabilize emotions.

PREHNITE

Love · Surrender · Healing · Detoxification · Acceptance

COLOR	green
CHAKRA	solar plexus and heart
ZODIAC SIGNS	Libra and Capricorn
ELEMENT	earth and water
CRYSTAL PAIRINGS	green aventurine, peridot, Libyan desert glass, lepidolite, scolecite, or emerald
PRECAUTIONS	Prehnite contains aluminum and can be toxic if ingested.
AFFIRMATION	I forgive all that has come before me and all that is yet to come.

Spiritual Healing

- Enhances angelic and spirit guide communication.
- Stimulates intuition and psychic abilities.
- Opens your heart to surrender to what is.
- Enhances more vivid dreams and recalling dreams.

Physical Healing

- Helps balance and heal the circulatory, digestive, urinary, and lymphatic systems.
- Can cleanse the body of all toxins.
- Helps alleviate nightmares, night terrors, and deep-rooted fears.
- Assists in uncovering and healing deep traumas that have developed into disease.
- Aids in boosting the metabolism.

Emotional Healing

- Brings union of the heart and the will.
- Helps release ego identification with past wounds.
- Is a stone of unconditional love, bringing peace and protection to the heart.
- Helps you accept yourself and others for exactly who you and they are.
- Helps you declutter your mind and motivates you to declutter your space.
- Opens your heart up to forgiving yourself and others.

EPIDOTE

Heart Opener · Positivity · Balance · Confidence
Emotional Stability

COLOR	green and white
CHAKRA	heart
ZODIAC SIGNS	Gemini and Libra
ELEMENT	earth and water
CRYSTAL PAIRINGS	herkimer diamond, nephrite jade, or moss agate
PRECAUTIONS	Epidote contains aluminum and can be toxic if ingested.
AFFIRMATION	I open my heart to receive unconditional love.

Spiritual Healing

- Brings in a balanced and stabilized energetic flow.

- Works to raise your vibrations.

- Encourages a sense of connection to mother nature, allowing you to be more present.

- Works to amplify and speed up your manifestations.

- Provides an energetic shield of protection from negative energy.

Physical Healing

- Works on finding healing and hope for those who struggle with an unknown physical disease.

- Helps those suffering from brain disorders such as Parkinson's, Alzheimer's, or dementia.

- May aid in the healing and balance of the digestive system.

- Helps calm and stabilize the nervous system.

- Supports a healthy thyroid, gallbladder, adrenal glands, and liver.

Emotional Healing

- Helps you get through emotional breakthroughs.

- Opens your mind and heart to understanding others' perspectives

- Allows emotional blocks to be released by opening your heart.

- Boosts personal power and self-confidence.

- Brings mental clarity, insightfulness, patience, and focus.

OCEAN JASPER

Happiness · Relaxation · Optimism
Self-Awareness · Safety

COLOR	all
CHAKRA	all
ZODIAC SIGNS	Capricorn, Virgo, Libra, and Scorpio
ELEMENT	earth and water
CRYSTAL PAIRINGS	agate, sunstone, golden healer, or opal
PRECAUTIONS	Never clean ocean jasper with household chemicals or leave it out in direct sunlight for hours because most ocean jasper contains quartz.
AFFIRMATION	I am a magnet for all things that bring me joy, positivity, and miracles.

Spiritual Healing

- Surrenders you to accepting love and light in the midst of darkness.

- Releases negative energy and replaces it with positivity.

- Helps you feel protected, secure, and safe.

- Helps you move forward and feel whole again by healing emotional and spiritual traumas.

- Promotes deep relaxation by reconnecting your spirit to earth and its healing vibrations.

Physical Healing

- Calms and soothes the nervous system.

- Works to strengthen and heal the physical heart.

- Helps bring the body back into its natural state and energetic rhythm.

- Assists in replenishing and restoring the adrenal glands when they have been on overdrive.

- Promotes cellular regeneration.

Emotional Healing

- Brings feelings of happiness and joy.

- Can assist individuals who are feeling depressed in regaining their enthusiasm for life.

- Enhances self-discovery and inner power.

- Can relieve stress and tension in the emotional body.

- Encourages you to be kind, empathetic, and understanding.

AGATE

Grounding · Awakening · Harmony · Connection · Release

COLOR	all
CHAKRA	all
ZODIAC SIGNS	Gemini
ELEMENT	earth
CRYSTAL PAIRINGS	smoky quartz, red jasper, ocean jasper, clear quartz, jet, or hematite
PRECAUTIONS	Never clean with household chemicals or leave out in the direct sunlight for hours because most agates contain quartz.
AFFIRMATION	I am grounded, protected, and balanced.

Spiritual Healing

- Brings good luck, protection, and fortune.
- Cleanses and expands your auric field.
- Increases spiritual awakening and growth.
- Brings balance and harmony to your mind, body, and spirit.
- Allows you to become more present in the moment by grounding and connecting to mother nature.

Physical Healing

- Promotes overall health and well-being.
- Helps you overcome any negative habits or addictions.
- Can aid in the relief of back pain caused by the avoidance of unpleasant feelings.
- Brings comfort and healing for the skin.
- Promotes peaceful sleep.

Emotional Healing

- Aids in the release of anger and tension in the body.
- Enhances mental clarity, focus, and attention to detail.
- Helps you feel safe and emotionally stable.
- Opens your heart up again to accept unconditional love.
- Promotes positivity, joy, and peace.

BLUE LACE AGATE

Serenity · Peace · Trust · Empathy · Relief

COLOR	baby blue
CHAKRA	throat
ZODIAC SIGNS	Gemini and Pisces
ELEMENT	air and water
CRYSTAL PAIRINGS	aquamarine, blue chalcedony, howlite, or lepidolite
PRECAUTIONS	none
AFFIRMATION	I experience a sense of peace and tranquility with every breath I take.

Spiritual Healing

- Promotes positive acceptance of everything that unfolds in your life.

- Can link your thoughts to calm a spiritual vibration, bringing you overall serenity.

- Connects us more closely to our spiritual guides, who can assist us in finding answers.

- Opens your heart up to trust yourself and others.

- Can help you connect to higher spiritual realms and consciousness.

Physical Healing

- Assists in the relief of sore throats, aching, congestion, and swollen glands.

- Can improve and promote healthy skin.

- Known to balance the thyroid and thymus glands.

- Promotes a good night's rest.

- Supports a healthy respiratory system.

Emotional Healing

- Promotes calming the mind, peace, and lightheartedness.

- Can help alleviate any anxiety, stress, or tension in the body.

- Helps you stay focused on the present moment, especially when you are stressed.

- Increases feelings of self-confidence and self-esteem.

- Helps maintain a level head, allowing for reasonable thinking.

TURQUOISE

Communication · Peace · Mindfulness
Kindness · Authenticity

COLOR	blue and green
CHAKRA	heart and throat
ZODIAC SIGNS	Sagittarius, Aquarius, Pisces, and Scorpio
ELEMENT	air and water
CRYSTAL PAIRINGS	amazonite, aquamarine, garnierite, or malachite
PRECAUTIONS	Turquoise contains aluminum and copper and can be toxic if ingested.
AFFIRMATION	I speak my truth with clarity and wisdom.

Spiritual Healing

- Helps you be mindful and live in the present moment.
- Allows the soul to open and express itself from a place of peace and love.
- Helps you remain on an enlightened path that is for your highest good.
- Encourages adaptation to change.
- Is known to bring good luck, protection, and fortune.

Physical Healing

- Helps oxygenate the blood and increase the amount of life force in the physical body.
- Aids in combating PTSD, depression, chronic fatigue, and anxiety.
- Helps maintain a healthy immune system.
- Works to decrease inflammation and tension in the body.
- Can alleviate pain, including menstrual cramps.

Emotional Healing

- Brings you back to the present moment, especially when you are stressed.
- Helps you articulate and bring forth your deepest authentic self.
- Helps you forgive others, accept yourself for who you are, and release regrets.
- Enlightens you so you can see love, light, compassion, kindness, and generosity within yourself and others.
- Promotes speaking your truth with integrity.

ANGELITE

Angelic Connection · Communication
Emotional Balance · Peace · Positivity

COLOR	blue
CHAKRA	throat, third eye, and crown
ZODIAC SIGNS	Aquarius
ELEMENT	wind
CRYSTAL PAIRINGS	celestite, herkimer diamond, amethyst, or aquamarine
PRECAUTIONS	Do not put angelite in water; it may dissolve.
AFFIRMATION	I am surrounded by pure love, support, protection, and light from my angels.

Spiritual Healing

- Awakens your spiritual connection to higher realms.
- Connects you to love, support, and protection from your angels.
- Enhances your meditation, positive affirmations, and intentions.
- Activates a greater sense of belonging in this world.
- Facilitates and induces the rebirthing process, the journey of spiritual awakening.

Physical Healing

- Promotes a peaceful night's rest provided by angels.
- Works to regulate and bring balance to the thyroid, the thymus, and throat infections.
- Supports healthy and strong bones.
- Can help maintain a healthy digestive system.
- Supports healthy water balance and fluid levels in the body.

Emotional Healing

- Encourages positive communication with others and yourself.
- Enhances confidence and honesty within yourself.
- Helps calm the mind, bringing feelings of peace and serenity.
- Aids in releasing negative self-talk, fears, and phobias.
- Helps bring a sense of peace and relief during times of grief.

AQUAMARINE

Calming · Tranquility · Soothing
Communication · Cooling

COLOR	green and blue
CHAKRA	throat and heart
ZODIAC SIGNS	Pisces and Aquarius
ELEMENT	water
CRYSTAL PAIRINGS	kunzite, morganite, emerald, chrysocolla, turquoise, or celestite
PRECAUTIONS	Aquamarine contains aluminum and can be toxic if ingested. It is sensitive to sunlight and intense temperature changes.
AFFIRMATION	I am flowing through life with ease, kindness, and inner peace.

Spiritual Healing

- Provides a deeper connection to your spirit guides and higher self.

- Promotes deep spiritual development and awareness.

- Clears stagnant energy in both the heart and throat chakras.

- Provides an energetic shield around the aura and subtle bodies.

- Assists in activating the memory to help you remember past-life experiences.

Physical Healing

- Works to minimize inflammation and swelling in the body.

- Assists in the healing of your nose, eyes, ears, and throat.

- Can reduce fevers by cooling the body.

- Promotes healthy skin and youthfulness.

Emotional Healing

- Brings feelings of inner peace and tranquility within.

- Enables you to be compassionate toward yourself and others.

- Helps you feel empowered and courageous.

- Aids you in overcoming grief and emotional traumas.

- Helps you release old negative thoughts and emotional patterns.

- Encourages you to speak your truth with clear communication.

CELESTITE

Peace · Angels · Serenity · Communication · Relaxation

COLOR	baby blue
CHAKRA	throat, third eye, and crown
ZODIAC SIGNS	Gemini and Cancer
ELEMENT	wind
CRYSTAL PAIRINGS	angelite, amethyst, clear quartz, aquamarine, blue chalcedony, or honey calcite
PRECAUTIONS	Do not keep celestite in direct sunlight, as the color will fade. Avoid using it in water, as the stone is very soft and may break into pieces.
AFFIRMATION	I release all doubts and welcome inner peace.

Spiritual Healing

- Helps you communicate with your higher self, angels, and spirit guides.
- Magnifies your spiritual awakening and experience.
- Attracts good luck and fortune.
- Stimulates clairvoyant communication.
- Helps you acknowledge and accept your spiritual gifts from the Divine.
- Works on releasing stuck energies in the aura, subtle bodies, and chakras.
- Harmonizes your yin and yang energies.

Physical Healing

- Brings peace, stillness, and harmony to the body.
- Aids in the treatment of the ears, mouth, head, nose, and throat.
- Aids in minimizing inflammation and pain in the body.
- Helps soothe and relieve any digestive issues.
- Promotes a peaceful night's rest.

Emotional Healing

- Helps combat any fears of flying, agoraphobia, speaking in public, or large crowds.
- Can relieve stress and anxiety.
- Helps maintain emotional balance and stability.
- Instills feelings of inner peace, serenity, hope, and tranquility.

CHRYSOCOLLA

Gentleness • Joy • Emotional Stability
Peace • Communication

COLOR	blue and green
CHAKRA	heart and throat
ZODIAC SIGNS	Sagittarius, Gemini, Virgo, and Taurus
ELEMENT	water
CRYSTAL PAIRINGS	aquamarine, azurite, or malachite
PRECAUTIONS	Chrysocolla contains copper and can be toxic if ingested. It is a soft stone that shouldn't be placed in water.
AFFIRMATION	I am able to express myself from a place of love and honesty.

Spiritual Healing

- Instills world and inner peace.
- Stimulates intuition and psychic abilities.
- Works to balance and connect to your divine femininity.
- Allows you to accept what is and go with the flow of life.
- Helps you become attuned to the earth's energetic healing vibrations.

Physical Healing

- Is beneficial during PMS symptoms, reducing menstrual cramps.
- Aids in releasing stress, anxiety, worry, and tension in the body.
- Supports a healthy thyroid, thymus, and respiratory system.
- Assists in replenishing and restoring the adrenal glands.
- Helps assist in the regulation of insulin and balancing blood sugar levels.

Emotional Healing

- Increases feelings of empathy toward others.
- Assists in recovering emotionally from a partner's abuse.
- Increases your capability to receive and give love.
- Helps banish guilt, which allows room for more joy and happiness.
- Encourages you to speak your truth by communicating from the heart.

AMAZONITE

Tranquility · Communication · Comfort · Truth · Health

COLOR	green and blue
CHAKRA	throat and heart
ZODIAC SIGNS	Virgo, Aquarius, and Pisces
ELEMENT	air and water
CRYSTAL PAIRINGS	aquamarine, chrysocolla, or turquoise
PRECAUTIONS	Do not use amazonite in an elixir because it contains copper.
AFFIRMATION	I am at peace with who I am today.

Spiritual Healing

- Soothes and rejuvenates all seven chakras.

- Illuminates and refills your aura.

- Helps you set boundaries with others.

- Boosts creativity and imagination.

- Enhances communication to help you speak and honor your truth.

Physical Healing

- Assists in the recovery process following a traumatic surgery or injury.

- Encourages a happy and healthy lifestyle.

- Helps bring the adrenal and thyroid glands back into balance after they are overworked because of anxiety or too much stress.

- Supports a healthy immune system.

- Works on strengthening the bones and joints.

Emotional Healing

- Opens the heart up again to receive love from others.

- Helps release and heal emotional trauma.

- Aids in calming a troubled mind.

- Promotes feelings of peace, joy, and serenity.

- Allows you to accept and understand your feelings with ease.

BLUE CHALCEDONY

Tranquility · Harmony · Transformation
Communication · Balance

COLOR	blue
CHAKRA	throat and third eye
ZODIAC SIGNS	Aquarius, Pisces, and Libra
ELEMENT	water
CRYSTAL PAIRINGS	blue lace agate, aquamarine, howlite, lapis lazuli, or celestite
PRECAUTIONS	none
AFFIRMATION	I let go of anything I cannot control and find inner peace within what I can control.

Spiritual Healing

- Supports balance of the mind, body, emotions, and spirit.
- Helps you communicate clearly through divine guidance.
- Aids in strengthening and repairing any energetic leaks in the aura.
- Facilitates a deeper meditation and inner channeling.
- Stimulates telepathic visions and psychic abilities.

Physical Healing

- Can help treat conditions of the female reproductive system.
- Works to cool the body to provide relief from throat inflammation and infections.
- Is a great stone for singers because it can strengthen your vocal cords.
- Promotes a deep and peaceful sleep.
- Can help treat conditions of the eyes, ears, nose, and respiratory system.

Emotional Healing

- Brings feelings of peace and tranquility while combating stress, nervousness, and anxiety.
- Helps you express your truth with love, comfort, and ease.
- Helps cool the body to release anger, tension, and fear that is emotionally stuck in the body.
- Boosts feelings of joy, optimism, and self-confidence.
- Allows you to release what no longer serves you so you can feel most at peace internally.

AMETHYST

Protection · Divinity · Intuition · Peace · Balance

COLOR	purple
CHAKRA	third eye and crown
ZODIAC SIGNS	Aquarius, Virgo, Capricorn, and Pisces
ELEMENT	air, water, and ether (spirit)
CRYSTAL PAIRINGS	All varieties of quartz, such as clear quartz, citrine, rose quartz, or smoky quartz. If you are using amethyst for protection, it pairs well with black tourmaline, jet, or black obsidian. If you are using it for recovering from addictions or negative thought patterns, kyanite is the perfect pairing.
PRECAUTIONS	Do not leave amethyst out in direct sunlight; the color will fade.
AFFIRMATION	I am connected and protected by divine light.

Spiritual Healing

- Is known as the "healer of people, animals, and plants."
- Provides protection from negative energy and psychic attacks.
- Boosts psychic gifts and intuition.
- Enhances meditation and connection to higher realms.
- Helps release any negative or stuck energies in the spiritual, physical, or emotional body.
- Works to stabilize and expand the aura.

Physical Healing

- Can be used to treat migraines and headaches.
- Supports overall health and well-being.
- Promotes a peaceful night's rest.
- Due to the high iron content, can help improve oxygen levels in the body.
- Helps calm the nervous system and bring it back into balance.

Emotional Healing

- Brings feelings of peace and harmony while combating stress and anxiety.
- Shifts negative thought patterns into positivity and optimism.
- Helps you recognize the root cause of your negative thoughts and behaviors.
- Helps you overcome any recurring negative bad habits, thought patterns, or addictions.

SUGILITE

Spiritual Wisdom · Confidence · Nurture
Deep Connection · Spiritual Protection

COLOR	purple
CHAKRA	third eye and crown
ZODIAC SIGNS	Virgo and Capricorn
ELEMENT	wind
CRYSTAL PAIRINGS	charoite, iolite, jet, or lapis lazuli
PRECAUTIONS	Sugilite contains aluminum and can be toxic if ingested. Putting it in direct sunlight should also be avoided because the color will fade.
AFFIRMATION	I deserve to be happy and successful.

Spiritual Healing

- Enables you to open your mind to all of life's endless possibilities.
- Is great for empaths and highly sensitive people, providing a sense of grounding and protection.
- Represents spiritual love, deep connection, and wisdom.
- Encourages you to live in the present moment.
- Helps clear out negative energy trapped in the aura, chakras, and meridians.

Physical Healing

- Can reduce migraines and headaches.
- Is known to boost endurance, vitality, and energy.
- Helps with all sleeping disorders, including nightmares.
- Due to the high iron content, can help improve oxygen levels and iron deficiencies in your body.
- Supports a healthy immune system and a healthy nervous system.

Emotional Healing

- Is a stone for mental balance, creativity, courage, and self-confidence.
- Aids in your ability to express yourself with ease, confidence, and flow.
- Can help with hostility, anger, jealousy, and forgiveness.
- Brings feelings of love, nurture, and care into your romantic relationships.
- Aids in releasing emotional blockages caused by trauma.

FLUORITE

Focus · Clarity · Divinity · Intuition · Protection

COLOR	green, purple, white, blue, pink, red, brown, and black
CHAKRA	heart, throat, third eye, and crown
ZODIAC SIGNS	Capricorn and Pisces
ELEMENT	wind
CRYSTAL PAIRINGS	amethyst, black tourmaline, labradorite, rose quartz, clear quartz, or moss agate
PRECAUTIONS	Do not put fluorite in direct sunlight; the color will begin to fade. Do not put it in water, as it can be toxic and dissolve.
AFFIRMATION	I am focused and concentrated on achieving my goals.

Spiritual Healing

- Provides an energetic shield to protect you from negative energy.

- Cleanses and restores all seven chakras.

- Protects, repairs, and seals the energy in the aura.

- Increases intuition, telepathy, and psychic abilities.

- Enhances and deepens your meditation.

Physical Healing

- Aids in the treatment of colds, flu, staph infections, or strep infections.

- Helps you feel more balanced, especially when experiencing vertigo.

- Aids in the mobility of joints.

- Aids in stimulating the mind, increasing concentration, focus, learning, and memory.

- Initiates cleansing and purification of the body's organs.

Emotional Healing

- Instills happy, healthy, and positive relationships with others.

- Works to balance the emotions and keep them stabilized.

- Calms the mind, reducing stress in the body.

- Encourages you to search within for answers instead of listening to outside influences.

- Awakens the mind to be open to endless opportunities.

LEPIDOLITE

Peace · Balance · Harmony · Healing · Tranquility

COLOR	purple
CHAKRA	heart and third eye
ZODIAC SIGNS	Libra, Virgo, Cancer, and Gemini
ELEMENT	earth and air
CRYSTAL PAIRINGS	blue lace agate, blue chalcedony, aquamarine, smoky quartz, hematite, amethyst, prehnite, or scolecite
PRECAUTIONS	Avoid placing lepidolite in water or in direct sunlight.
AFFIRMATION	I am in control of my thoughts and happiness

Spiritual Healing

- Aids in astral travel and rebirth.
- Helps you live in the present moment.
- Helps you move beyond your ego to altruism.
- Releases spiritual "baggage" and limiting beliefs.
- Provides assistance during big transitions in your life.
- Can be used to locate energy blockages within your body.

Physical Healing

- Helps you fall and stay asleep at night.
- Supports a healthy digestive system and metabolism.
- Helps balance the nervous system by soothing the nerves.
- Helps people with ADD and ADHD become more present and focused.
- Can increase flexibility in the joints.

Emotional Healing

- Aids in relieving anxiety, stress, depression, worry, and distrust.
- Opens your heart to love, forgiveness, and acceptance.
- Helps release trapped emotional anger, tension, and trauma.
- Works on balancing the emotions.

CHAROITE

Intuition · Protection · Positivity · Spirituality · Boundaries

COLOR	purple and black
CHAKRA	root, solar plexus, heart, third eye, and crown
ZODIAC SIGNS	Sagittarius, Pisces, and Scorpio
ELEMENT	wind
CRYSTAL PAIRINGS	sugilite, amethyst, moldavite, kunzite, jet, black tourmaline, shungite, or tiger's eye
PRECAUTIONS	none
AFFIRMATION	I am grounded, I am safe, and I am fully protected everywhere I go.

Spiritual Healing

- Releases lack of harmony and negative energy in the body.

- Stimulates intuition and psychic abilities.

- Brings high spiritual energy into union with unconditional love, which allows you to fully release and connect to your higher power.

- Allows you to deepen your meditation.

- Provides an energetic protection from toxic people, psychic attacks, and negative energies.

Physical Healing

- Works to build up your physical strength and mobility.

- Helps regulate a healthy blood pressure and heart rate.

- Aids in healing the liver, kidneys, digestive tract, spleen, and pancreas.

- Helps alleviate aches and pains in the body.

- When taken as an elixir, can help cleanse and purify the body.

Emotional Healing

- Helps you set healthy boundaries with others.

- Promotes compassion and empathy.

- Promotes inner reflection and encourages a positive outlook on any situation.

- Aids in opening the heart to forgiving yourself and others.

- Helps ground and stabilize the emotional body.

ROSE QUARTZ

Unconditional Love · Forgiveness · Compassion
Self-Love · Joy

COLOR	pink
CHAKRA	heart
ZODIAC SIGNS	Gemini and Taurus
ELEMENT	water
CRYSTAL PAIRINGS	morganite, emerald, rhodochrosite, rhodonite, amethyst, carnelian, fluorite, garnierite, green aventurine, kunzite, or thulite
PRECAUTIONS	Rose quartz will fade in direct sunlight.
AFFIRMATION	I love myself unconditionally.

Spiritual Healing

- Immerses the mind, body, and soul with the highest vibration, love.

- Deepens your connection with angels and angelic realms.

- Enhances affirmations that are repeated during meditation.

- Helps cleanse the emotional body of the aura.

Physical Healing

- Helps bring physical healing and strength to all areas of the heart.

- Helps men and women get through their mid-life crises.

- Aids in the treatment of any chest, lungs, or thymus imbalances.

- Can increase fertility, passion, and romance with your partner.

- Supports healthy circulation, reproductive organs, and skin.

Emotional Healing

- Is known to boost feelings of unconditional love for yourself and others.

- Promotes feelings of kindness, compassion, empathy, and generosity.

- Aids in recovery from abuse and heartbreak.

- Is known to increase feelings of overall happiness and joy.

- Helps bring a sense of peace and relief during times of grief.

- Opens the heart to allow you to forgive others and release the emotional trauma that's blocking the heart from wanting or receiving love.

RHODONITE

Love · Positive Relationships · Emotional Balance
Trauma · Healing · Self-Esteem

COLOR	pink and white
CHAKRA	heart
ZODIAC SIGNS	Scorpio and Taurus
ELEMENT	fire and earth
CRYSTAL PAIRINGS	rose quartz, rhodochrosite, morganite, or scolecite
PRECAUTIONS	Do not keep rhodonite in direct sunlight; the color will fade. Avoid using it in water, as the stone is softer and may crack or break.
AFFIRMATION	I use my gifts to fulfill my soul's purpose.

Spiritual Healing

- Can provide healing for emotional and past-life trauma.
- Aids you in living your life to the fullest and with self-actualization.
- Harmonizes feminine and masculine energies.
- Helps you understand your purpose in life and your spiritual life path.
- Encourages spiritual growth and transformation.

Physical Healing

- Can treat infertility and PMS symptoms.
- Supports weight loss and detoxification.
- Can help men and women through menopause.
- Supports a healthy immune system.
- Aids in reducing inflammation in the body.

Emotional Healing

- Aids in the relief of anxiety, stress, mental unrest, and confusion.
- Promotes healthy relationships and helps bond families closer together.
- Promotes feelings of unconditional love, self-esteem, and self-love.
- Helps clear energetic blockages that stem from past emotional wounds and scars.
- Promotes emotional balance and stability.

RHODOCHROSITE

Unconditional Self-Love • Deep Healing • Kindness
Forgiveness • Empathy

COLOR	pink and white
CHAKRA	heart
ZODIAC SIGNS	Scorpio, Taurus, Cancer, and Pisces
ELEMENT	fire and water
CRYSTAL PAIRINGS	rose quartz, emerald, eudialyte, morganite, rhodonite, or thulite
PRECAUTIONS	Do not keep rhodochrosite in direct sunlight; the color will fade. Avoid using it in water, as the stone is very soft and may break into pieces.
AFFIRMATION	My needs and feelings are valid.

Spiritual Healing

- Energizes and brings balance to the heart chakra.
- Assists in the healing of childhood trauma and past lives.
- Enhances your creativity, sparking new ideas and explorations.
- Renews passion and excitement for life.
- Emits the strongest vibration in the universe, love. It shows us the true meaning of unconditional love.

Physical Healing

- Can increase libido, physical energy, and sensuality.
- Aids in healthy development for babies.
- Brings the nervous system back into balance.
- Helps stimulate the mind and boosts memory.
- Supports a healthy spleen, heart, kidney, and circulation.

Emotional Healing

- Boosts feelings of unconditional love for yourself and others.
- Promotes feelings of courage, love, forgiveness, confidence, kindness, and compassion.
- May bring repressed feelings and trauma to the surface to be healed.
- Enables you to express yourself from the heart.
- Provides emotional stability and balance.

MORGANITE

Love · Compassion · Emotional Balance
Angelic Guidance · Surrender

COLOR	pink
CHAKRA	heart
ZODIAC SIGNS	Taurus and Cancer
ELEMENT	earth and water
CRYSTAL PAIRINGS	aquamarine, garnierite, green aventurine, kunzite, malachite, rose quartz, rhodochrosite, ruby, emerald, peridot, rhodonite, or thulite
PRECAUTIONS	Morganite contains aluminum and can be toxic if ingested. It is sensitive to sunlight and intense temperature changes.
AFFIRMATION	Divine love enters through the light of my heart.

Spiritual Healing

- Allows you to open your heart to angelic guidance and love.
- Surrenders you to accepting love and light in the midst of darkness.
- Allows you to trust your spirit guides and feel their support.
- Helps you reach self-actualization and alignment with your higher self in this lifetime.

Physical Healing

- Helps strengthen the physical heart and provide support during a heartbreak.
- Boosts inner and physical strength.
- Aids in the treatment of asthma, emphysema, and tuberculosis.

Emotional Healing

- Helps you be receptive to love from others and less protective of your heart.
- Helps you recognize and heal old emotional patterns of judgment, fear, self-hatred, or manipulation.
- Brings feelings of peace, support, and love during times of grief.
- Provides emotional protection and balance.
- Boosts feelings of joy, patience, confidence, and compassion.
- Encourages positive and loving relationships, both romantically and in friendships.

EUDIALYTE

Self-Love · Forgiveness · Uplifting · Healing
Spiritual Discovery

COLOR	pink, red, white, and black
CHAKRA	root and heart
ZODIAC SIGNS	Taurus, Aries, and Virgo
ELEMENT	earth and water
CRYSTAL PAIRINGS	rhodochrosite, ruby, or black tourmaline
PRECAUTIONS	Eudialyte is a soft stone and slightly radioactive. Do not put it in water.
AFFIRMATION	I fully open my heart to love myself and others.

Spiritual Healing

- Assists you in discovering your life's path.
- Purifies and protects you from negative energies.
- Helps you connect deeper to find answers from your spirit guides.
- Keeps you grounded and aligned with goals.
- Sparks creativity and new ideas.

Physical Healing

- Helps you become more present and loving in your physical body.
- Helps calm and stabilize the nervous system.
- Works with the body to help it self-heal.
- Aids in treating problems in the pancreas, thyroid, and eyes.
- Helps stabilize, balance, and heal the heart.

Emotional Healing

- Helps you overcome fears, self-doubt, and self-criticism.
- Opens the heart to forgiving others and loving yourself unconditionally.
- Provides a blanket of love when you are going through the grieving process.
- Helps uplift your mood on days when you feel down.
- Promotes healing from childhood abuse and trauma.

KUNZITE

Unconditional Love · Compassion · Expression
Flow · Emotional Healing

COLOR	pink and purple
CHAKRA	heart
ZODIAC SIGNS	Taurus, Leo, and Scorpio
ELEMENT	water
CRYSTAL PAIRINGS	aquamarine, charoite, emerald, garnierite, morganite, or rose quartz
PRECAUTIONS	Kunzite contains aluminum and can be toxic if ingested. It is sensitive to sunlight and intense temperature changes.
AFFIRMATION	I release outer influences and am filled with divine love.

Spiritual Healing

- Removes negative energy and acts as a protective shield around your auric field.

- Is highly vibrational, exuding divine love and light.

- Helps you release energy blockages in the heart, allowing you to become more open to love again.

- Induces a deep meditative state.

- Provides a blanket of love, helping you feel safe and secure.

Physical Healing

- Helps relieve heartache and heartbreak.

- Helps calm the nervous system.

- Keeps the body in flow, healing the circulatory system and blood pressure.

- Enhances femininity and female sexuality.

- Helps strengthen and regulate a healthy heart.

Emotional Healing

- Brings in feelings of unconditional love, self-love, expression, and flow.

- Promotes calmness, self-esteem, and control.

- Can relieve depression, anxiety, and stress.

- Helps release fears to let you experience life with joy and love.

- Helps you open your heart up to love again.

RUBY

Passion · Love · Vitality · Sexuality · Courage

COLOR	red and magenta
CHAKRA	root and heart
ZODIAC SIGNS	Aries and Leo
ELEMENT	earth and fire
CRYSTAL PAIRINGS	sapphire, eudialyte, garnet, morganite, peridot, or thulite
PRECAUTIONS	Ruby contains aluminum and can be toxic if ingested. It is sensitive to sunlight and intense temperature changes.
AFFIRMATION	I am grounded and present.

Spiritual Healing

- Helps you ground to the physical world.
- Activates the meridians and Kundalini energy.
- Strengthens your life force (prana) and chi throughout the body.
- Opens your heart to feeling and connecting with divine love.
- Provides an energetic loving shield of protection over the heart chakra.

Physical Healing

- Aids in bringing circulation and energy flow to the feet and legs.
- Helps stimulate vitality, energy, and burning passion for life.
- Boosts libido and sexual energy and can help you overcome infertility.
- Helps you become more focused, attentive, and aligned.
- Aids in recovering from any addictions, abuse, or childhood trauma.

Emotional Healing

- Helps you express love toward yourself.
- Brings enthusiasm and openheartedness for life.
- Is a stone of courage, helping you become comfortable with the unknown.
- Boosts emotional strength, stability, balance, and stamina.
- Increases passion and lust for your romantic partner.

THULITE

Love · Pleasure · Generosity · Deep Healing · Compassion

COLOR	pink and red
CHAKRA	sacral, solar plexus, heart, and throat
ZODIAC SIGNS	Gemini and Taurus
ELEMENT	wind and water
CRYSTAL PAIRINGS	rhodochrosite, ruby, morganite, or rose quartz
PRECAUTIONS	Thulite contains aluminum and can be toxic if ingested.
AFFIRMATION	I am constantly in the vibration of love.

Spiritual Healing

- Stimulates healing and regeneration within your life force.
- Aids in speeding up and amplifying your manifestations.
- Opens the heart chakra for deep healing to be activated.
- Enlightens you on your true soul purpose in this lifetime.

Physical Healing

- Has a strong healing ability to regenerate and heal the body.
- Stimulates sexual energy and libido.
- Works to clear any reproductive issues that have stemmed from past abuse.
- Brings vitality, energy, and restoration for your health and is especially beneficial for those struggling with chronic fatigue.
- Helps increase physical balance and coordination.

Emotional Healing

- Encourages happiness, pleasure, passion, affection, and enthusiasm.
- Helps maintain good relationships, find new compatible friends, and initiate a romantic relationship.
- Helps us rest the pains of our past and move forward with compassion for ourselves and others.
- Opens the heart to unconditional love for yourself and others.
- Aids in overcoming detrimental addictions that make you feel unworthy of a wonderful life.

BLACK TOURMALINE

Grounding · Protection · Purification · Positivity · Connection

COLOR	black
CHAKRA	root
ZODIAC SIGNS	Libra, Scorpio, and Capricorn
ELEMENT	earth
CRYSTAL PAIRINGS	jet, smoky quartz, selenite, hematite, amethyst, black obsidian, eudialyte, larvikite, moldavite, black onyx, shungite, or charoite
PRECAUTIONS	Black tourmaline may contain aluminum and can be toxic if ingested.
AFFIRMATION	My mind, body, and spirit are protected and filled with infinite light.

Spiritual Healing

- Repels, deflects, and protects you from negative energy.
- Works to release stagnant energy in your aura, chakras, or subtle bodies.
- Cleanses and removes toxic energy and replenishes it with energy from the earth.
- Increases spiritual growth and abundance.
- Facilitates speeding up your manifestations.
- Connects you deeply to mother nature, allowing you to feel more grounded and centered.

Physical Healing

- Can reduce pain and numbness.
- Protects you from harmful radiation from electromagnetic fields (EMFs).
- Aids in the detoxification of the body of all poisons and chemicals.
- Supports a healthy immune system and adrenal glands.
- Works to increase physical vitality and energy.

Emotional Healing

- Encourages cooperation and optimism.
- Helps reduce stress, anxiety, and worried thoughts.
- Supports a healthy emotional state and stability.
- Can reduce or eliminate suicidal thoughts and excessive fear.

BLACK OBSIDIAN

Protection · Grounding · Purification
Acceptance · Positivity

COLOR	black
CHAKRA	root
ZODIAC SIGNS	Scorpio and Capricorn
ELEMENT	earth
CRYSTAL PAIRINGS	black tourmaline, howlite, jet, smoky quartz, black onyx, or petrified wood
PRECAUTIONS	none
AFFIRMATION	I am divinely protected from all negative energy and shielded by beaming white light.

Spiritual Healing

- Provides an energetic shield, protecting you from negative energy.

- Connects you to the spiritual world to heal past-life issues.

- Works to remove any negative attachments stuck in the energy field.

- Encourages you to find your soul purpose.

- Grounds you into your body and mother nature.

- Sparks creativity and imagination.

Physical Healing

- Can alleviate pain and tension in the body.

- Aids in regulating a healthy digestive system and metabolism.

- Works to heal any reproductive issues that have stemmed from past abuse.

- Supports a healthy flow of blood in the body.

Emotional Healing

- Helps you conquer issues relating to past misuse of personal power.

- Works to release negative beliefs about yourself.

- Helps you feel empowered enough to take control and responsibility for your own healing.

- Enhances your capacity to exercise self-control and resist temptation to achieve your goals.

- Helps you overcome any recurring negative bad habits, thought patterns, or addictions.

SHUNGITE

EMF Protection · Grounding · Vitality · Purification · Balance

COLOR	black
CHAKRA	root
ZODIAC SIGNS	Scorpio, Capricorn, and Cancer
ELEMENT	fire, wind, and storm
CRYSTAL PAIRINGS	smoky quartz, black tourmaline, hematite, black onyx, copper, charoite, or nephrite jade
PRECAUTIONS	Shungite is a soft stone but is safe in water.
AFFIRMATION	I live my life fearlessly.

Spiritual Healing

- Provides protection against negative energy in the body or home.

- Promotes grounding and connection to earth's healing and nourishing energies.

- Purifies and balances the body, yin and yang energies, and chakras.

- Provides direction to help you fulfill your soul purpose in this lifetime.

- Acts as a catalyst for spiritual growth and transformation.

Physical Healing

- Provides protection against any harmful environmental energies that affect your physical body.

- Works to increase physical energy and stamina, relieving fatigue and insomnia.

- Purifies your water (when using elite shungite).

- Is known to absorb and eliminate any health hazards.

- Protects you from harmful radiation from electromagnetic fields (EMFs).

- Supports a healthy digestive system, skin, and immune system.

Emotional Healing

- Helps calm an overactive mind, releasing panic, worry, fear, stress, stuck emotions, and anxiety.

- Helps calm the mind to achieve ultimate peace and harmony.

- Aids in releasing aggressive energy and fills your energy with love.

BLACK ONYX

Intention · Protection · Grounding · Strength
Personal Power

COLOR	black
CHAKRA	root, solar plexus, and third eye
ZODIAC SIGNS	Taurus and Scorpio
ELEMENT	earth
CRYSTAL PAIRINGS	black tourmaline, black obsidian, rainbow moonstone, or shungite
PRECAUTIONS	Do not put black onyx out in the sun for a prolonged period.
AFFIRMATION	I release all negativity from my mind, body, and soul.

Spiritual Healing

- Enhances protection from negative energy.
- Helps you ground yourself to mother nature.
- Enhances spiritual vision and dream experiences.
- Amplifies your intentions and allows you to think clearly.
- Harmonizes masculine and feminine energies.

Physical Healing

- Boosts the retention of memory and encourages attention to detail.
- Can increase physical strength, vitality, and stamina.
- Helps you release any unwanted excess energy.
- Can calm and soothe the nervous system.
- Aids in the treatment of disorders related to the feet, bone marrow, and tissues.

Emotional Healing

- Assists in boosting personal power, inner strength, and willpower.
- Brings forth a calm state of mind in heated situations.
- Helps you create a more structured, controlled, and disciplined life.
- Helps release any anger or anxiety stuck in your emotional body.
- Encourages positivity and happiness.

JET

Rejuvenation · Protection · Purification
Stress Relief · Positivity

COLOR	black
CHAKRA	root
ZODIAC SIGNS	Gemini, Aries, and Taurus
ELEMENT	earth
CRYSTAL PAIRINGS	black obsidian, black tourmaline, amber, amethyst, bloodstone, charoite, hematite, lepidolite, sugilite, or serpentine
PRECAUTIONS	Do not put jet in water; it is a very soft, brittle stone.
AFFIRMATION	My mind, body, and spirit are grounded, centered, and purified.

Spiritual Healing

- Provides protection against negative energy in the body or home.

- Clears the energy field of negative attachments and addictive patterns.

- Assists in awakening your psychic awareness and gifts.

- Can stimulate financial abundance and business success.

- Deepens your meditation and raises your Kundalini energy.

Physical Healing

- Energetically cleanses and rejuvenates the liver and kidneys.

- Helps ease pain from migraines, upset stomach, and the flu.

- Is beneficial during PMS symptoms, reducing menstrual cramps.

- Aids in the treatment of epilepsy, colds, and lymphatic swelling.

Emotional Healing

- Lets you see the lessons in negative experiences and helps you integrate those lessons.

- Helps bring emotional balance and stability.

- Helps you step into your personal power and full potential.

- Helps alleviate depression, bringing that spark back into your life, filling it with joy and love.

- Can reduce stress and worried thinking.

- Aids in reducing depression, anxiety, and unwanted fears.

HERKIMER DIAMOND

High Vibrational · Amplifier · Protector · Dreamer
Mental Clarity

COLOR	clear and white
CHAKRA	third eye and crown
ZODIAC SIGNS	Libra, Scorpio, and Sagittarius
ELEMENT	air
CRYSTAL PAIRINGS	all, especially moldavite
PRECAUTIONS	Herkimer diamond's color will fade, and it can cause a fire when in direct sunlight.
AFFIRMATION	I am constantly radiating love and light.

Spiritual Healing

- Infuses more energetic light into the body to help you feel full of light at all times.

- Is a stone of dreams and vision work.

- Assists in removing energetic cords or negative patterns.

- Amplifies all energies, crystals, and intentions.

- Assists highly spiritual people in enjoying the physical world.

- Promotes lucid dreaming and astral traveling.

- Can be utilized to attune yourself with another person, place, or activity.

- Enhances your intuition and psychic abilities.

Physical Healing

- Aids in purifying and cleansing the physical body.

- Helps boost the immune system.

- Provides a layer of protection from physical burnout.

- Boosts one's overall physical energy and stamina.

Emotional Healing

- Aids in clearing the mind of unconscious fears and repressions.

- Assists you in achieving self-actualization, where your life's full potential is reached.

- Facilitates healing and overall emotional well-being.

CLEAR QUARTZ

Master Healer · Divinity · Spirituality
Manifestor · Amplification

COLOR	clear
CHAKRA	crown
ZODIAC SIGNS	all
ELEMENT	air, water, and fire
CRYSTAL PAIRINGS	all
PRECAUTIONS	Clear quartz is sensitive to light and can cause a fire when in prolonged direct sunlight.
AFFIRMATION	I honor and accept the Divine within me.

Spiritual Healing

- Is used to amplify crystals, the physical body, energy, thoughts, and intentions.

- Provides an energetic shield of protection against negative energy.

- Facilitates the manifestation process.

- Repairs leakages and expands your auric field.

- Known as the "master healer" because of its ability to be programmed to work on any physical, mental, emotional, or spiritual ailment.

- Facilitates communicating and connecting with your higher consciousness and spirit guides.

- Increases clarity in understanding your intuition or psychic messages better.

- Helps clear and activate all energy centers of the body.

Physical Healing

- Has the ability to work with any health condition in the body to help bring it back into balance.

- Brings vitality, energy, and restoration for your health.

- Supports a healthy nervous system and immune system.

Emotional Healing

- Helps stimulate the mind and boost your memory.

- Works with emotional energy to stimulate positive feelings.

- Helps treat any mental or emotional disorders.

- Aids in releasing negative emotional attachments to others.

LEMURIAN

Healing · Divinity · Highly Vibrational
Manifestation · Expansion

COLOR	white and clear
CHAKRA	crown
ZODIAC SIGNS	Gemini
ELEMENT	wind and storm
CRYSTAL PAIRINGS	all
PRECAUTIONS	Lemurian is sensitive to light and can cause a fire when in direct sunlight.
AFFIRMATION	I am a beacon of healing love and light.

Spiritual Healing

- Expands your inner light.
- Helps speed up the manifestation process.
- Helps improve your quality of life.
- Is perfect for using during Reiki healing sessions or any energy work.
- Connects you to your spirit guides, angels, and higher self.
- Promotes karmic healing and removal of negative attachments.

Physical Healing

- Supports a healthy heart, brain, immune system, and nervous system.
- Can minimize inflammation and pain in the body.
- Aids in a speedy recovery after a surgery, bruise, injury, or physical trauma.
- Has the ability to work with any health condition in the body to help bring it back into balance.

Emotional Healing

- Brings greater connection so you can see and love your authentic self.
- Calms the mind, bringing peace and tranquility.
- Can provide healing from emotional trauma.
- Provokes feelings of love, nurture, and connection.
- Helps you feel emotionally connected and understand that you aren't ever alone in this world.

HOWLITE

Calm · Peace · Awareness · Restful Sleep · Bone Strength

COLOR	white and gray
CHAKRA	crown
ZODIAC SIGNS	Virgo, Gemini, and Cancer
ELEMENT	air
CRYSTAL PAIRINGS	lepidolite, black obsidian, or scolecite
PRECAUTIONS	Howlite contains boron and can be toxic if ingested. It is a soft stone, so do not submerge it in water.
AFFIRMATION	I am at peace and harmony with everyone and everything.

Spiritual Healing

- Allows you to deepen your meditation.
- Provides a deep insight into your past lives.
- Helps you find your authentic self.
- Facilitates connecting to your higher consciousness, realms, and awareness.
- Absorbs negative energy.

Physical Healing

- Can provide pain relief.
- Is great for keeping in your nightstand or under your pillow at night for a peaceful sleep.
- Helps stimulate the mind and improve memory.
- Is great for strengthening the bones, teeth, and soft tissues.

Emotional Healing

- Helps stabilize your emotions.
- Assists in motivation and ambition for reaching your goals.
- Can help quiet and calm the mind, increasing relaxation.
- Aids in reducing frustration, anxiety, tension, worries, stress, and anger.
- Removes the possibility of becoming conceited or self-centered.
- Encourages emotional expression.

RAINBOW MOONSTONE

New Beginnings · Insight · Femininity · Balance
Divine Connection

COLOR	white and black with flashes of blue
CHAKRA	sacral and crown
ZODIAC SIGNS	Gemini, Cancer, Scorpio, and Libra
ELEMENT	water and ether (spirit)
CRYSTAL PAIRINGS	labradorite, garnierite, azurite, herkimer diamond, moldavite, black onyx, or opal
PRECAUTIONS	Do not keep rainbow moonstone exposed to prolonged sunlight.
AFFIRMATION	I embrace the positive changes to come with open arms.

Spiritual Healing

- Stimulates intuition, insight, and creativity.
- Provides spiritual guidance to help you find your purpose.
- Provides protection when working with lucid dreaming of visionary quests.
- Helps you go through change and new beginnings with ease and excitement.
- Provides protection and repairs any leakages in the auric field.
- Can offer protection and provide good fortune when you are traveling.

Physical Healing

- Helps heal any imbalances in the digestive tract.
- Eases menopause and premenstrual symptoms.
- Helps women with fertility, childbirth, hormonal imbalances, and sexuality issues.
- Supports healthy ears, skin, hair, eyes, and organs.
- Provides connection between the physical, emotional, and spiritual bodies.

Emotional Healing

- Boosts feelings of self-confidence, optimism, joy, and hope.
- Aids in releasing anger, frustration, and irritability.
- Brings peace, calmness, and composure to the mind.
- Helps you understand your emotions from a place of love and promotes emotional well-being.
- Encourages feelings of love, compassion, and understanding.

SELENITE

Spiritual Guidance · Physical Healing · Protection
Harmony · Authenticity

COLOR	white and clear
CHAKRA	crown
ZODIAC SIGNS	Cancer, Scorpio, Pisces, and Taurus
ELEMENT	air and water
CRYSTAL PAIRINGS	all
PRECAUTIONS	Do not put selenite in prolonged sunlight. It is a very soft stone; do not put it in water.
AFFIRMATION	I release any negative energy that no longer serves my highest good.

Spiritual Healing

- Provides access to understanding and connecting to your past and future lives.

- Provides a bright, energetic white light shielding your auric field and your home.

- Enhances telepathy, intuition, and clairvoyant sensations.

- Connects you to angelic guidance and communication.

- Cleanses and charges all other crystals.

- Enhances meditation and connection to higher realms.

Physical Healing

- Can alleviate pain, inflammation, and tension in the body.

- May clear blockages that initiate physical healing.

- Promotes a healthy balanced nervous system.

- On a cellular level, can counteract the effects of free radicals to heal and restore.

- Supports a healthy spine and alignment.

Emotional Healing

- Helps you recognize your best and most authentic self.

- Helps you stay mentally focused and alert, reducing mental fog.

- Helps calm the mind to promote inner peace and a sense of tranquility.

- Aids in emotional balance and stability.

SCOLECITE

Soothing · Inner Peace · Awareness · Harmony
Spiritual Connection

COLOR	white
CHAKRA	third eye and crown
ZODIAC SIGNS	Capricorn
ELEMENT	wind and ether (spirit)
CRYSTAL PAIRINGS	prehnite, rhodonite, howlite, azurite, lepidolite, selenite, or sodalite
PRECAUTIONS	Scolecite is a soft stone; do not put it in water. Prolonged sun exposure may damage the crystal.
AFFIRMATION	I am always at a state of peace and harmony.

Spiritual Healing

- Brings a sense of tranquility, inner peace, and serenity that can gently lift you to higher planes of awareness.

- Enhances your dream state; is great for lucid dreaming.

- Awakens the heart when connecting to your spirit.

- Helps you receive spiritual inspiration and insight.

- Connects you to higher spirit realms, your higher self, spirit guides, other dimensions, and extraterrestrials.

- Provides spiritual guidance to help you find your soul purpose in this lifetime.

Physical Healing

- Helps support proper serotonin levels, to keep one happy and joyful throughout the day.

- Promotes a deep and restful sleep.

- Helps empaths and introverts recharge their energy after being drained by others.

- Supports a healthy digestive system, spine, lungs, eyes, and circulatory system.

Emotional Healing

- Clears mental "debris" so your true inner light can shine.

- Helps you stay balanced and calm when faced with difficult situations.

- Brings feelings of peace and harmony while combating stress and anxiety.

- Boosts feelings of self-love and self-confidence.

- Promotes compassion and empathy.

PYRITE

Fool's Gold · Good Luck · Confidence
Abundance · Manifestation

COLOR	gold
CHAKRA	solar plexus
ZODIAC SIGNS	Leo and Gemini
ELEMENT	earth
CRYSTAL PAIRINGS	citrine, lapis lazuli, green aventurine, or nephrite jade
PRECAUTIONS	Do not put pyrite in water; it can fade in color or rust.
AFFIRMATION	Money comes to me easily and effortlessly.

Spiritual Healing

- Provides an energetic shield to protect you from negative energy.

- Gives you a sense of safety, security, stability, and grounding.

- Helps increase your vibration and speed up the manifestation process.

- Magnifies your attraction to prosperity, good luck, and abundance.

Physical Healing

- Supports a healthy endocrine system.

- Helps stimulate the mind and enhances memory recall.

- Helps heal the digestive system and boost metabolism.

- Works to purify the body of infection, toxins, and diseases.

- Supports a healthy male reproductive system, especially in regard to impotence and infertility.

Emotional Healing

- Assists in overcoming deep, profound fears.

- Can help you become more motivated and ambitious.

- Strengthens your personal power and assertiveness.

- Boosts feelings of self-confidence, courage, and self-worth.

- Encourages healthy and positive relationships.

HEMATITE

Protection · Grounding · Connection · Positivity · Balance

COLOR	black
CHAKRA	root
ZODIAC SIGNS	Aquarius
ELEMENT	earth
CRYSTAL PAIRINGS	agate, black tourmaline, black obsidian, shungite, or jet
PRECAUTIONS	Do not submerge hematite in water; it can rust.
AFFIRMATION	I am grounded, centered, and balanced.

Spiritual Healing

- Harmonizes your yin and yang energies.
- Balances the mind, body, and spirit.
- Provides an energetic shield protecting you from negative energy.
- Is one of the most powerful stones for grounding into mother nature's healing energies, allowing you to become more present in the moment.
- Helps you identify your inner strengths and limitations so that you may use them to improve, conquer, and succeed on all levels.

Physical Healing

- Aids in detoxifying the liver and organs.
- Accelerates the body's natural healing process.
- Provides protection against harmful electromagnetic fields (EMFs).
- Assists in the absorption of iron and formation of red blood cells.
- Promotes healthy blood flow and circulatory system.

Emotional Healing

- Instills strength, ambition, love, and courage.
- Helps release judgment of yourself and others.
- Helps you remember your ideas and memories.
- Assists in releasing negative habits and addictive thought patterns.
- Facilitates the attainment of inner peace and happiness.

SMOKY QUARTZ

Protection · Grounding · Peace · Balance
Restoration of Energy

COLOR	black, brown, and white
CHAKRA	root
ZODIAC SIGNS	Capricorn, Scorpio, Taurus, and Virgo
ELEMENT	earth
CRYSTAL PAIRINGS	agate, black obsidian, amethyst, black tourmaline, lepidolite, or red jasper
PRECAUTIONS	The color of a smoky quartz will fade or change due to prolonged sun exposure.
AFFIRMATION	I am grounded and present in the moment at all times.

Spiritual Healing

- Helps cleanse the aura and chakras of any blockages.
- Provides a shield of protection from negative energies.
- Harmonizes your yin and yang energies.
- Is grounding, reconnecting you to the earth's healing energy.
- Deepens your meditation, allowing for clear thoughts and the ability to be more present in the moment.

Physical Healing

- Helps bring the body back into equilibrium.
- Can relieve chronic pain, including migraines and cramps.
- After an illness, can restore vitality and physical energy.
- Protects you from harmful radiation from electromagnetic fields (EMFs).
- Promotes a restful night's sleep.

Emotional Healing

- Works to reduce anxiety, stressful thoughts, panic attacks, and self-harm thoughts.
- Calms the mind, so it is perfect for use during meditation.
- Can release negative thoughts associated with fear, jealousy, or anger.
- Supports mental clarity and emotional balance.
- Is known to increase cooperation and unification with others so you can reach the same goal or desire.

PETRIFIED WOOD

Transformation · Earthiness · Security · Balance · Energy

COLOR	brown, red, white, black, purple, and orange
CHAKRA	root and sacral
ZODIAC SIGNS	Leo, Virgo, Capricorn, Taurus, and Scorpio
ELEMENT	earth
CRYSTAL PAIRINGS	moss agate, black obsidian, or red jasper
PRECAUTIONS	none
AFFIRMATION	I embrace transformation.

Spiritual Healing

- Is grounding, reconnecting you to the earth's energy.
- Helps you become aligned with your ultimate purpose in this lifetime.
- Helps release any stuck or scattered energies.
- Provides a foundation for new goals, transformation, or changing of your life path.
- Provides access to and understanding of your past lives.

Physical Healing

- Can help improve your overall physical health and well-being.
- Works to strengthen the bones and joints.
- Boosts physical vitality and energy in the body.
- Works on healing the organs in the sacral chakra.

Emotional Healing

- Teaches patience and understanding of how to go with the flow of life.
- Helps release feelings of stress and worry.
- Increases passion and joy for life.
- Helps bring balance to your emotional well-being.
- Promotes feelings of safety and security.

TIGER'S EYE

Courage · Open-Mindedness · Strength
Good Luck · Grounding

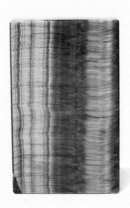

COLOR	brown and yellow
CHAKRA	root and solar plexus
ZODIAC SIGNS	Aries and Capricorn
ELEMENT	fire and earth
CRYSTAL PAIRINGS	malachite, septarian, serpentine, or charoite
PRECAUTIONS	Do not submerge tiger's eye in water. It is toxic if ingested.
AFFIRMATION	I am filled with warmth, courage, and strength.

Spiritual Healing

- Is great for boosting intuition, psychic processes, spiritual awakening, and intuitive impressions.

- Brings good luck and prosperity.

- Provides protection against negative energy.

- Is grounding, providing a deeper connection to mother earth.

- Harmonizes yin and yang energy.

Physical Healing

- Helps heal from an injury or broken bone.

- Helps with all sleeping disorders, including nightmares or night terrors.

- Can reduce unhealthy and addictive cravings.

- Works to increase physical energy, strength, and vitality.

- Supports healthy adrenal glands, reproductive system, and vision.

Emotional Healing

- Promotes open-mindedness.

- Brings a sense of balance, harmony, and inner peace.

- Helps combat fear, worry, and depression.

- Gives you courage, especially when you're starting anything new.

- Can strengthen your personal power, self-discipline, and confidence.

SHIVA LINGAM

Balance · Fertility · Kundalini Energy Awakening
Enlightenment · New Beginnings

COLOR	brown
CHAKRA	all
ZODIAC SIGNS	Scorpio, Aries, and Cancer
ELEMENT	earth, wind, water, fire, and storm
CRYSTAL PAIRINGS	carnelian or clear quartz
PRECAUTIONS	none
AFFIRMATION	I bring balance and serenity to every aspect of my life.

Spiritual Healing

- Awakens Kundalini energy, starting at the base of the spine and spiraling upward.
- Balances feminine and masculine energies.
- Awakens the auric field, igniting the "fire" within.
- Symbolizes primeval energy of the creator, god, or higher power.
- Opens and balances all seven chakras.
- Awakens and deepens your connection to higher consciousness.

Physical Healing

- Can treat infertility and imbalances in the reproductive system.
- Is known to boost libido in both sexes.
- Aids in increasing physical strength and vitality.
- Helps improve overall health and well-being.

Emotional Healing

- Helps remove unwelcome sexual tension.
- Assists in overcoming fearful and negative thinking.
- Welcomes new beginnings and encourages fresh ideas and solutions.
- Can help release negative thoughts and judgments of others.
- Can aid in opening your heart to compassion and empathy for others.

COPPER

Optimism · Energy · Purification · Healing · Amplifier

COLOR	copper
CHAKRA	all
ZODIAC SIGNS	Taurus and Sagittarius
ELEMENT	earth and water
CRYSTAL PAIRINGS	all
PRECAUTIONS	Do not put copper in water. It is toxic if ingested.
AFFIRMATION	I am spiritually connected to manifest anything I desire.

Spiritual Healing

- Connects you between heaven and earth, making it perfect for amplifying your manifestations.

- Can clear out all negative energy and rebalance all seven chakras.

- Conducts and magnifies the energies surrounding it.

- Provides an energy protection shield.

- When used with other crystals, amplifies and purifies their healing properties.

- Brings good luck and prosperity.

Physical Healing

- Can boost libido, energy, stamina, and vitality.

- Aids in relieving pain from broken bones, rheumatism, and arthritis.

- Helps boost the immune system and fight off infectious diseases.

- Works to keep the body in flow, which can improve circulation and oxygen levels.

- Can stabilize and balance blood flow.

- Helps maintain overall health and wellness.

Emotional Healing

- Helps combat unacceptance of yourself by bringing self-love and optimism to the surface.

- Can strengthen personal power and self-esteem.

- Helps us align with our soul purpose and true inner potential.

BLUE APATITE

Restoration · Communication · Longevity
Psychic Awareness · Vitality

COLOR	blue
CHAKRA	throat and third eye
ZODIAC SIGNS	Gemini
ELEMENT	wind
CRYSTAL PAIRINGS	amethyst, carnelian, lapis lazuli, or citrine
PRECAUTIONS	Do not submerge blue apatite in water or keep it in direct sunlight for long periods of time; the color will fade.
AFFIRMATION	My body deserves love, support, and respect

Spiritual Healing

- Enhances psychic abilities and intuition.
- Helps clear out karma and negativity from your past and present.
- Awakens the third-eye chakra to help you dive deep into understanding your past life, Akashic records, and soul purpose.
- Stimulates lucid dreaming and astral travel.
- Deepens your meditation and raises your Kundalini energy.
- Harmonizes your yin and yang energies.

Physical Healing

- Helps with vertigo and dizziness by restoring the body's natural state of balance.
- Stimulates vitality, energy, and youthfulness.
- May suppress appetite and curb cravings to assist with weight loss.
- Supports a healthfully functioning heart.
- Supports healing of the organs and glands energetically.

Emotional Healing

- Promotes inner clarity, mental clarity, and self-insight.
- Works to improve overall feelings of self-worth and self-confidence.
- Helps you speak your truth with confidence in a social setting.
- Promotes a positive mindset, especially when it comes to thoughts about your body.

IOLITE

Intuition · Expansion · Insight · Meditation · Life Path

COLOR	indigo blue
CHAKRA	third eye
ZODIAC SIGNS	Sagittarius, Pisces, and Cancer
ELEMENT	air and water
CRYSTAL PAIRINGS	amethyst, azurite, sodalite, sugilite, sunstone, lapis lazuli, or sapphire
PRECAUTIONS	Iolite contains aluminum and can be toxic if ingested. Avoid putting it in prolonged direct sunlight, as the color may begin to fade.
AFFIRMATION	I trust in my own actions and intuition.

Spiritual Healing

- Awakens the third-eye chakra and psychic gifts.

- Recharges and expands the auric field.

- Facilitates intuitive insight and visualization.

- Helps strengthen the energetic bond between the heart and brain, to find deep feelings of peace and joy.

- Supports deep meditation, dreaming, and visualization.

Physical Healing

- May help ease the pain of headaches and eye strain.

- Stimulates the memory to prevent memory loss.

- Helps you fall asleep and stay asleep at night.

- Helps detoxify and regenerate the liver.

- Supports the eyes, nervous system, and respiratory system.

Emotional Healing

- Can calm an overactive mind to help you reach a state of meditation.

- Helps you gain emotional distance and find a clearer perspective on any life situation.

- Helps you uncover the lost part of yourself and offers you the chance to take your inner path to your deep self.

- Aids in diminishing fears of the unknown.

- Eases the need to be perfect and have control over every little thing.

SODALITE

Communication · Intuition · Concentration
Self-Expression · Harmony

COLOR	blue and white
CHAKRA	throat and third eye
ZODIAC SIGNS	Virgo and Libra
ELEMENT	earth and water
CRYSTAL PAIRINGS	iolite, lapis lazuli, blue sapphire, or scolecite
PRECAUTIONS	Avoid putting sodalite in prolonged sunlight; the color will fade.
AFFIRMATION	I am staying true to myself despite judgment from others.

Spiritual Healing

- Stimulates lucid dreaming.
- Provides deep spiritual insight and direction into understanding your most authentic self.
- Helps you move beyond your ego to a state of altruism.
- Enhances intuition and psychic abilities.
- Increases spiritual development and awareness.

Physical Healing

- Can balance blood pressure and flow.
- Aids in memory stimulation and the reduction of mental fog.
- Aids in treating any digestive disorders.
- Supports a healthy lymphatic system, immune system, and vocal cords.
- Promotes deeper sleep and helps reduce insomnia.

Emotional Healing

- Works to calm the mind and balance emotions.
- Helps you release anger and trapped emotions.
- Provides mental clarity so you can speak rationally and truthfully.
- Can promote self-expression, speaking your truth, and enhanced communication.
- Increases self-esteem and self-trust.

LAPIS LAZULI

Wisdom · Awareness · Deep Connection · Intuition · Goddess

COLOR	blue, gold, and gray
CHAKRA	throat and third eye
ZODIAC SIGNS	Libra and Sagittarius
ELEMENT	wind
CRYSTAL PAIRINGS	blue apatite, iolite, blue chalcedony, pyrite, sugilite, larvikite, blue sapphire, or sodalite
PRECAUTIONS	Do not put lapis lazuli in water; it contains aluminum and is toxic to ingest.
AFFIRMATION	I am divinely guided and protected at all times.

Spiritual Healing

- Boosts psychic abilities and intuition.
- Brings you to a higher awareness of yourself.
- Enhances visualization and deep connection during meditation.
- Helps provide you with deeper insight and answers about your past life.
- Assists in spiritual expansion, awakening, awareness, and realization of consciousness.
- Helps you learn from and understand your spiritual experiences.

Physical Healing

- Helps relieve insomnia, vertigo, and dizziness.
- Enhances higher cognitive thinking.
- Can reduce pain and inflammation in the body.
- Supports healthy endocrine, nervous, and immune systems.

Emotional Healing

- Can help you overcome depression.
- Brings inner peace, mental balance, and tranquility.
- Aids in relaxation and healthy relationships.
- Encourages mental endurance, wisdom, self-acceptance, and creativity.
- Supports emotional and mental clarity.

KYANITE

Positive Thoughts · Balance · Communication
Spiritual Guidance · Tranquility

COLOR	Blue
CHAKRA	throat and third eye
ZODIAC SIGNS	Taurus, Sagittarius, Pisces, and Cancer
ELEMENT	storm, water, and air
CRYSTAL PAIRINGS	amethyst, clear quartz, labradorite, or selenite
PRECAUTIONS	Do not put kyanite in water. It contains aluminum and is a very brittle stone.
AFFIRMATION	Today, I replace old, negative habits with positive ones.

Spiritual Healing

- Facilitates a deep meditative state.
- Harmonizes the masculine and feminine energies.
- Is highly vibrational, bringing you into greater connection with your spirit guides.
- Strengthens intuition and understanding of that "gut feeling."
- Helps bring the chakras and layers of the aura into balance.

Physical Healing

- Can help support the throat, muscles, and brain.
- Aids in treating conditions of the sensory organs.
- Improves memory.
- Promotes recovery from a stroke, improving speech, coordination, and mobility.
- Provides overall balance for the nervous system.

Emotional Healing

- Is known for bringing calmness and tranquility.
- Helps release feelings of remorse and regret.
- Encourages mental stamina and positive communication.
- Assists in overcoming any negative bad habits, recurring thought patterns, or addictions.
- Helps release anger, frustration, and tension in the emotional body.

AZURITE

Intuition · Visionary · Clarity · Divinity · Personal Discovery

COLOR	dark blue
CHAKRA	third eye and crown
ZODIAC SIGNS	Pisces, Aquarius, and Gemini
ELEMENT	wind
CRYSTAL PAIRINGS	malachite, chrysocolla, fluorite, amethyst, rainbow moonstone, scolecite, iolite, or sapphire
PRECAUTIONS	Azurite contains copper and can be toxic if ingested. Do not place it in direct sunlight; the color will begin to fade.
AFFIRMATION	I fully trust my inner guidance.

Spiritual Healing

- Stimulates psychic ability and intuition.
- Helps you find a greater connection with your higher self.
- Works to strengthen the astral and etheric bodies, providing protection from the negative energies of others.
- Strengthens your auric field.
- Provides a way to deepen and awaken your meditation with ease.
- Helps ignite diving deep into your past lives to promote spiritual healing.
- Is known as the "stone of heaven" and provides deep guidance to the heavenly self.

Physical Healing

- Helps heal all issues in the brain and head, such as headaches, vertigo, and tinnitus.
- Supports a healthy liver, thyroid, and nervous system.
- Helps clear toxins from the body.

Emotional Healing

- Helps you dive deep into the root cause of your greatest fears and how to seek love over fear.
- Helps you understand others' true motives instead of assuming the worst.
- Provides a gateway for deep self-discovery.
- Aids in breaking free of being judgmental toward others.
- Stimulates the release of limiting beliefs.

LABRADORITE

Transformation · Intuition · Expansion
Protection · Revelation

COLOR	gray with flashes of blue, pink, purple, green, yellow, and orange
CHAKRA	throat, third eye, and crown
ZODIAC SIGNS	Leo, Scorpio, and Sagittarius
ELEMENT	water and air
CRYSTAL PAIRINGS	rainbow moonstone, fluorite, kyanite, clear quartz, sunstone, or larvikite
PRECAUTIONS	Labradorite contains aluminum and can be toxic if ingested.
AFFIRMATION	I welcome change and transformation into my life with open arms.

Spiritual Healing

- Stimulates your imagination, intuition, and psychic abilities.
- Provides a protective energetic shield from negative or evil energies around you.
- Is a stone of transformation, helping you overcome obstacles to reach your destiny.
- Encourages spiritual development and awareness.
- Helps you recognize and see your inner light.

Physical Healing

- Can reduce high blood pressure.
- Aids in the treatment of disorders of the eyes and brain.
- Can alleviate stress and anxiety in the body.
- Can help you discover the root cause of why you may have developed a physical disease or illness.
- Helps release pain or inflammation from the body.
- Supports healthy digestion, regulation, and metabolism.

Emotional Healing

- Helps reduce social anxiety and impulsive behavior.
- Assists in overcoming fear-based thinking.
- Boosts self-confidence, imagination, harmony, and mental clarity.
- Helps you release negative thoughts about yourself that are stored in your subconscious mind.

LARVIKITE

Inner Strength • Positivity • Greater Connection
Intuition • Peace

COLOR	deep blue, black, and silver
CHAKRA	root, throat, and third eye
ZODIAC SIGNS	Aquarius
ELEMENT	earth
CRYSTAL PAIRINGS	lapis lazuli, black tourmaline, amethyst, or labradorite
PRECAUTIONS	Larvikite contains aluminum and can be toxic if ingested.
AFFIRMATION	My inner strength moves mountains.

Spiritual Healing

- Can repel negative energy.

- Stimulates intuition and psychic abilities.

- Can refract the energies surrounding you that usually make you feel off or imbalanced.

- Connects you to your higher self.

- Helps ground and connect you to earth's healing energy.

- Increases your sense of security and inner strength.

Physical Healing

- Encourages youthfulness and vitality.

- Helps balance hormones.

- Helps you recover from a stroke, improving speech, brain function, and mobility.

- Assists in calming the nervous system.

- Helps initiate the cleansing and purification of the body's tissues.

Emotional Healing

- Can clear your mind of cluttered and unwanted thoughts.

- Works on giving you the inner strength to overcome emotional battles.

- Reduces stress or worried thinking.

- Stimulates attention to detail and focus.

BLUE SAPPHIRE

Awareness · Intuition · Self-Discovery
Communication · Focus

COLOR	blue
CHAKRA	throat and third eye
ZODIAC SIGNS	Capricorn, Aquarius, and Virgo
ELEMENT	wind and earth
CRYSTAL PAIRINGS	ruby, lapis lazuli, iolite, azurite, or sodalite
PRECAUTIONS	Blue sapphire contains aluminum and can be toxic if ingested. It is sensitive to sunlight and intense temperature changes.
AFFIRMATION	I am constantly speaking my truth.

Spiritual Healing

- Is a great stone for meditation, bringing you into a deeper state of consciousness and awareness.
- Stimulates the lucid dream state.
- Boosts psychic abilities and intuition.
- Helps you find a greater connection with your higher self.
- Helps release negative attachments with your ego to achieve altruism.

Physical Healing

- Helps heal headaches, eye problems, inner ear imbalances, and vertigo.
- Can strengthen the mind, increase learning, and increase focus.
- Balances the thyroid and thymus glands.
- Helps calm the nervous system.
- Helps detoxify and purify the body, making it great for supporting weight loss.

Emotional Healing

- Helps you find your own voice, if you are easily persuaded.
- Activates determination, discipline, and motivation.
- Can strengthen your love life and help you let go of any insecurities you have with your significant other.
- Provides a gateway for deep discovery of yourself.
- Helps improve mental clarity, strength, and focus.

OPAL

Beauty · Imagination · Emotional Release
Angels · Good Luck

COLOR	rainbow
CHAKRA	all
ZODIAC SIGNS	Virgo, Scorpio, and Libra
ELEMENT	water and air
CRYSTAL PAIRINGS	herkimer diamond, citrine, opal, rainbow moonstone, or lemurian
PRECAUTIONS	Most opals have a high water content, so exposure to bright light for extended periods can cause breakage or cracks. Most opals need to be submerged in water so they don't crack.
AFFIRMATION	I allow my emotional healing to begin.

Spiritual Healing

- Instills the aura with a frequency of joy.
- Enhances imagination and creativity.
- Balances and aligns all seven chakras.
- Expands your life force and angelic connection.
- Is known to bring good luck and fortune.
- Helps you embrace change with open arms.

Physical Healing

- Helps provide relief from skin disorders such as eczema, psoriasis, and rosacea.
- Can bring the kidneys back into healthy alignment.
- Aids in strengthening hair, nails, and skin.
- Supports a healthy female reproductive system.

Emotional Healing

- Promotes beauty, inside and out.
- Helps you release your anger, fears, self-doubt, wounds, and negativity.
- Helps you become more positive and loving.
- Helps you to release what no longer serves you, so you can begin your emotional healing.
- Promotes emotional balance and stability.

INDEX OF CRYSTALS

AGATE	70		COPPER	150
BLUE LACE AGATE	72		EMERALD	50
MOSS AGATE	56		EPIDOTE	66
AMAZONITE	84		EUDIALYTE	106
AMBER	42		FLUORITE	92
AMETHYST	88		GARNET	24
ANGELITE	76		GARNIERITE	54
BLUE APATITE	152		GOLDEN HEALER	34
AQUAMARINE	78		HEMATITE	140
GREEN AVENTURINE	52		HERKIMER DIAMOND	124
AZURITE	162		HOWLITE	130
BLOODSTONE	48		IOLITE	154
HONEY CALCITE	38		NEPHRITE GREEN JADE	44
CARNELIAN	28		OCEAN JASPER	68
CELESTITE	80		RED JASPER	22
BLUE CHALCEDONY	86		JET	122
CHAROITE	96		KUNZITE	108
CHRYSOCOLLA	82		KYANITE	160
CITRINE	32		LABRADORITE	164

INDEX OF CRYSTALS

LAPIS LAZULI	158	RHODOCHROSITE	102
LARVIKITE	166	RHODONITE	100
LEMURIAN	128	RUBY	110
LEPIDOLITE	94	BLUE SAPPHIRE	168
LIBYAN DESERT GLASS	36	SARDONYX	30
MALACHITE	46	SCOLECITE	136
MOLDAVITE	58	SELENITE	134
RAINBOW MOONSTONE	132	SEPTARIAN	40
MORGANITE	104	SERPENTINE	62
BLACK OBSIDIAN	116	SHIVA LINGAM	148
BLACK ONYX	120	SHUNGITE	118
OPAL	170	SODALITE	156
PERIDOT	60	SUGILITE	90
PETRIFIED WOOD	144	SUNSTONE	26
PREHNITE	64	THULITE	112
PYRITE	138	TIGER'S EYE	146
CLEAR QUARTZ	126	BLACK TOURMALINE	114
ROSE QUARTZ	98	TURQUOISE	74
SMOKY QUARTZ	142		

ACKNOWLEDGMENTS

To my husband and soulmate, Joel Hancock, thank you deeply for being my rock through everything. You have always reminded me in my darkest days that there was a greater purpose out there for me, I just have to move through the darkness and into the light to see it. I am so beyond grateful to have you by my side through it all. You have helped make this dream of mine come to life in so many ways. Thank you for helping me with the book photography, loving support, and guidance. I love you so very much. Together, we are able to help the lives of so many through our crystal company, Lovingthyselfrocks, and I hope to do the same with this book.

To my Lovingthyselfrocks team (friends and family), Mom, Hannah (sister), Kelsey, Billy, Mark, and Marco, thank you for believing in me since day 1. The love and passion you have to help change people's lives through crystals and love, inspires me daily. Your support, love, kindness, and hard work is deeply appreciated from the bottom of my heart. Our company wouldn't be possible without each and every one of you. You all mean the world to me, and I am forever grateful to not only have you as part of the LTR team, but as my family.

To Lisa Toney, I am beyond grateful to have been blessed by the guidance of the Universe that led me to you. You were the first person who introduced me to my spiritual journey, energy work, and crystals. This book wouldn't have been possible without you. I am so grateful to have you as a friend and spiritual mentor.

To Diane Pilatovsky, I am so blessed that the Universe led me to you. You have helped me through the darkness moments of my life and helped me learn so much about my own spiritual journey, energy work, personal growth, and unconditional love for self.

Thank you from the bottom of my heart, writing this book wouldn't have been possible without you.

To my *Lovingthyselfrocks* community, I am forever grateful for all of your love and support. You have made this book opportunity possible. Thank you for your loving, kind, and caring messages daily that have allowed me to strengthen my knowledge and understanding on how crystals have helped heal you in ways that I could share with readers in this book. Your healing has made a ripple effect on not only your life, my life, but anyone who reads this book. Thank you deeply.

To Ashley Leavy from Love and Light School of Crystal Therapy, thank you for your deep love and passion for sharing your knowledge and healing about crystals. I am forever grateful to have gotten my Advanced Crystals Practitioner Certification from your program. You're such a light to this world.

To Jill and the entire Quarto Publishing Team, thank you for this incredible opportunity to write and publish *The Ultimate Guide to Crystals* and *The Crystal Companion*. Each and every one of you have made this book possible and I am forever grateful for your kindness, hard work, guidance, and passion.

To all my guides and mentors, thank you for guiding me into the light of who I really am. I am forever grateful to have found and love who I am and share my life's purpose with the world. Each and every one of you has a special place in my heart and I am so blessed that the Universe led me to you.

To all of my friends and family, it's been such a joy seeing all of you step into the love and light that you are. Thank you for your loving support for our crystal company *Lovingthyselfrocks* and the writing of this book. I love each and every one of you.

ABOUT THE AUTHOR

Rachel Hancock is a Certified Advanced Crystal Practitioner and Reiki Master and holds a bachelor's degree in Physical and Health Science with a minor in psychology. She, along with her husband Joel, is the founder of *Lovingthyselfrocks*, one the top crystal purveyors and crystal education sites on Instagram. Founded in 2018, *Lovingthyselfrocks* has sold hundreds of thousands of crystals to customers around the world and is located in Winter Park, Florida, as well as online. Rachel's mission is to promote the power of self-love and healing crystals.